Computer Science

Pure and Simple

Book 2

for Homeschoolers

by Phyllis Wheeler & Don Sleeth

Motherboard
Books

Table of Contents

Introduction v
More on MicroWorlds 2.0 and EX vii
Part 1: MicroWorlds Games 1
   #1 Review of Procedures, Input, and Variables 3
   #2 Madlibs 13
   #3 Madlibs II 21
   #4 Review of Animation Using Variables 25
   #5 The Wandering Turtle 29
   #6 Enhanced Wandering Turtle 37
   #7 Maze I 42
   #8 Maze II: Win or Lose? 51
   #9 Maze III 57
   #10 Maze IV 63
   #11 Get Ready, Get Set for Race 66
   #12 Race II 67
   #13 Race III 72
   #14 Hangman I: Going Loopy 73
   #15 Hangman II 79
   #16 Hangman III 87
   #17 Hangman IV 92
   #18 City I 94
   #19 City II 100
   #20 City III 103
Part II: Internet Exercises 105
   #21 Internet Scavenger Hunt: Animals 107
   #22 Internet Scavenger Hunt: Geography 110
   #23 Web Page Brush-Up 111
   #24 Web Page I 117
   #25 Web Page II 118
   #26 Web Page III 121
   #27 Putting Your Site on the Web 126
Part III: Various Programming Skills 129
   #28 Using a Spreadsheet for Calculations 131
   #29 Procedures, or Functions, in a Spreadsheet 136
   #30 The Next Step: DOS 143
   #31 Where from Here? 152
Appendices 156
   Appendix I: MicroWorlds Troubleshooting and Procedure Names 157
   Appendix II: HTML Troubleshooting and Commands 159
   Appendix III: Bibliography 161
   Appendix IV: Answers 162
Index 174

About the Authors

Phyllis Wheeler taught computer science in a homeschool co-op in St. Louis. Now a homeschooling mother, she has worked in the aerospace industry as a mechanical engineer. Along the way she has written some computer programs and taken some computer courses. She has also worked as a newspaper reporter and free-lance writer. She has bachelor's degrees in English from Smith College and in mechanical engineering from Washington University in St. Louis.

Don Sleeth is a computer professional in Canada who wrote a manuscript of lessons to teach his daughter programming with MicroWorlds Logo. His contributions to this book are included in the MicroWorlds review and the Wandering Turtle lessons.

Acknowledgments

In many ways our homeschool co-op computer class and the books that resulted have been a collaborative effort. I would like to acknowledge the contributions of:

- Steven Sittser, who donated his time to provide computer lab time for the students in the evening. He helped me work out some solutions to the game problems and provided expertise on DOS, Web site hosting, and other subjects.

- John A. Sparks, also known as Gio, who made all this possible through generous donations of his time to set up and maintain our homeschool computer lab.

- Clayton Community Church, which has gone out of its way to support the co-op and the computer lab.

- The students in my classes, including Hannah Wheeler (age 16 when she took this class) and Paul Wheeler (age 11 when he took this class), for their ideas on zany ways to add to the games I proposed.

Phyllis Wheeler

Introduction

Kids really enjoy creating and embellishing computer games, as we found at our co-op as our kids worked away on these projects. Partly it's the challenge, and partly it's the creative process. Each youngster's creation is unique and something to really be proud of. Moreover, this fun subject is useful. It teaches logical thinking and provides a job skill for the future, a time when computers will surely be even more indispensable than they are now. As with any subject, the younger the students are introduced, the more comfortable they are with the subject as adults. *Computer Science Pure and Simple* books seek to bring programming concepts to children as young as fifth grade. They are intended for use with an adult who knows something about computers—how to open a Word processor, how to use email, and how to install programs.

Computer Science Pure and Simple Book 1 provides an introduction to MicroWorlds Logo programming, the Internet and related HTML programming, and office skills for kids in fifth grade and up. This book, *Book 2*, is aimed more at youngsters in seventh through twelfth grades, although a younger child who is interested could handle most of the work. It provides a brief review of beginning Logo programming followed by five detailed games. These are old standbys Madlibs, Maze, and Hangman and new inventions City and Race. *Book 2* also provides a brushup on HTML and then moves on to more complex Web site design using a free "What You See Is What You Get" editor, Mozilla Composer. Then *Book 2* teaches some spreadsheet programming, an introduction to DOS, and a lead-in to other books that teach the C language.

This book grew out of the efforts of a homeschool co-op in St. Louis, Missouri. It represents a transcription of our efforts to teach intermediate computer skills to second-year computer students during the course of a year, meeting once a week. I made adjustments for what worked well and what didn't. So the curriculum has been tested!

Troubleshooting

For the homeschool teacher, computer expertise is not required, although some experience as a computer user is desirable. We provide an answer key in the back of the book. We suggest that you let your student puzzle over a problem for a while before handing out some hints and then finally, if necessary, letting him see the answer. To troubleshoot programs that don't work, look for suggestions in the text and at the troubleshooting guides for HTML and MicroWorlds in the Appendix. LCSI, the software provider, also provides technical support at www.microworlds.com.

You Need a MicroWorlds Disk

You will need a copy of MicroWorlds 2.0 or EX software to use this book. If you don't have a copy, get one at www.Motherboardbooks.com (MW 2.0 for home users at a discount), or at www.microworlds.com (MW 2.0 and EX, school or home use, full price). MicroWorlds teaches programming using the Logo computer language. MicroWorlds does our job admirably:

- Using graphics, it instantly shows young programmers the results of their efforts. It makes computer science fun instead of difficult.

- It introduces students to the universal elements of computer languages, including variables and logic. Once students learn one computer language, it will be easy to pick up another.

- MicroWorlds 2.0 will work on older computers as well as newer ones. MicroWorlds EX is also available. This is essentially the same program, all formatted on one page instead of two, with higher resolution graphics.

- Visual Basic provides a similar result and is used in the workplace. But this Microsoft application is more complex to learn and costs considerably more than MicroWorlds.

- There are inexpensive or free computer applications out there, but they don't provide the programming result in a graphic form. We feel this graphic result is vital to grab and keep kids' interest.

Internet Safety for Children

This book asks students to search for information on the Internet, which is full of inappropriate content. At the least, you the parent should sit with your student while they are searching the Internet. But there is much more you can do to provide them with independence in using this marvelous and dangerous tool. You can install parental controls on your computer through your Internet Service Provider (such as AOL, SBC Global, or Earthlink), or you can install a separate filter. A filter usable with DSL or dialup is www.SafeEyes.com.

You can direct your search engine to look only at safe sites. Lesson 21 directs the student to set the filter in Google to SafeSearch. To get an even more restrictive search engine, you can use www.SurfSafely.com. SurfSafely limits searching to Web sites whose creators have certified that they pose no threat to children (unfortunately not a large proportion of the safe sites that are out there). You can get further information on how to allow your children to use the Internet safely at www.getnetwise.org. Look for the Tools menu. Another site with a variety of information is www.missingkids.com.

Minimum Computer Requirements

This course was designed with a PC in mind, running Microsoft Word, Microsoft Excel, a browser (Internet Explorer or Netscape) and MicroWorlds. We also suggest a free download of a PC Web page editor, Mozilla Composer. If you have a Macintosh with PC emulation, you should be able to follow the book as well. MicroWorlds will install on a Macintosh.

Here are **MicroWorlds 2.0** requirements:

PC: Windows 95/98/NT/Me/2000/XP
     486DX processor or Pentium
     16 MB RAM
     CD-ROM drive

Mac: Operating System 7.0 & higher
     16 MB RAM
     CD-ROM drive

Here are **MicroWorlds EX** requirements:

PC: Windows 98/NT/Me/2000/XP
     Pentium processor or higher
     32 MB RAM
     CD ROM drive

Mac: Macintosh OS X 10.2.8
     256 Mb of RAM
     CD ROM drive

More on MicroWorlds 2.0 and EX

This book was written with MicroWorlds 2.0 in mind. However, it would be easy to use MicroWorlds EX instead, and possibly other software that uses the Logo computer language, such as Terrapin Logo.

In MicroWorlds 2.0, you must click on the **Pages** menu at the top of the screen, and then click on Procedures. You are presented with a blank page. This is where as much of your code as possible belongs. You can toggle back and forth between the Procedures Page and Page1 where the turtle is drawing by pushing **ctrl** and **f** at the same time.

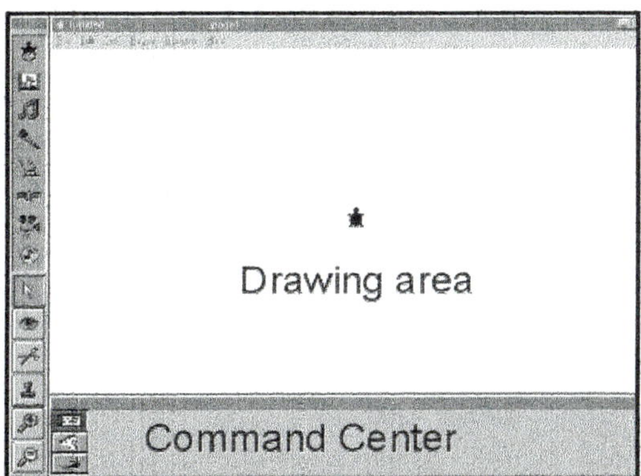

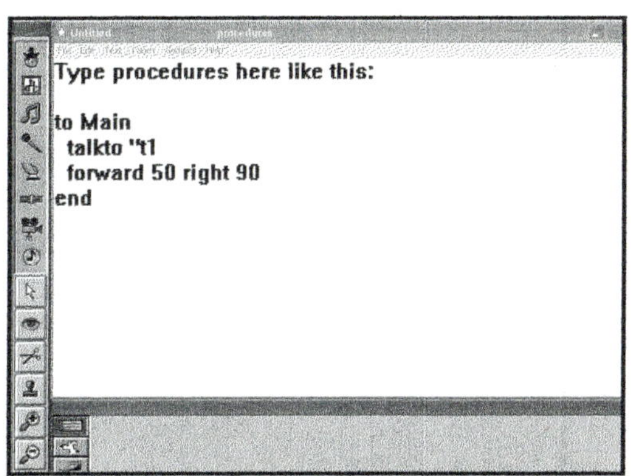

MicroWorlds 2.0 Graphics screen on left. Use Pages menu at the top to go to the Procedures Page, which looks similar!

You access the Shapes Center by clicking on the dog's head to the left of the Command Center. You access the Drawing Center by clicking on the paintbrush icon to the left of the Command Center. **You use the Command Center to try out individual lines of code, or to call a procedure that you have written on the Procedures Page.** Return to the Command Center by clicking on the icon above the dog's head. Other useful icons are on the left side of the screen. When you open the Shapes Center, you see a variety of predrawn shapes, plus some blanks that you can use to create your own, if you double click on the blank.

In MicroWorlds EX, the Procedures "Page" or window is to the right alongside the Graphics "Page," provided the Procedures tab beneath it is selected. The Command Center is to the bottom left.

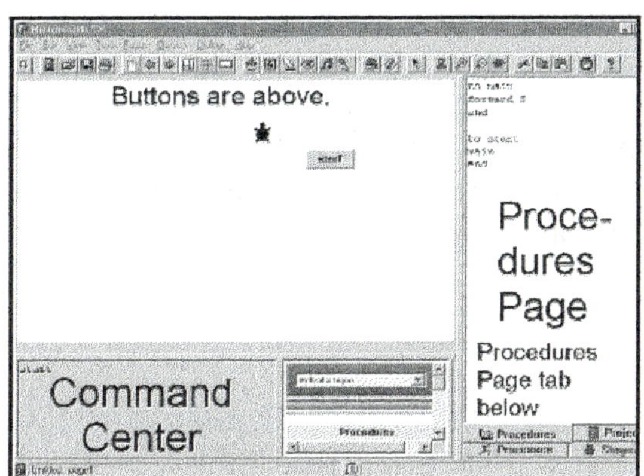

You access the Shapes Center by clicking on the **Shapes** tab below the Procedures Page section. You will need to import shapes from the drawing/painting window to your Shapes Center before using any non-turtle shapes. Click on the icon at the top that looks like a yellow pad with paintbrush. The drawing/painting/clipart window opens up. Click on the daisy icon to see the single shapes or the two-people icon to see animation shapes. Now drag the drawing window over to the left by clicking down on the blue band at the top, and holding the mouse button down, dragging sideways. Make sure the window on the right is the shape center by clicking on the tab beneath it that says **Shapes**.

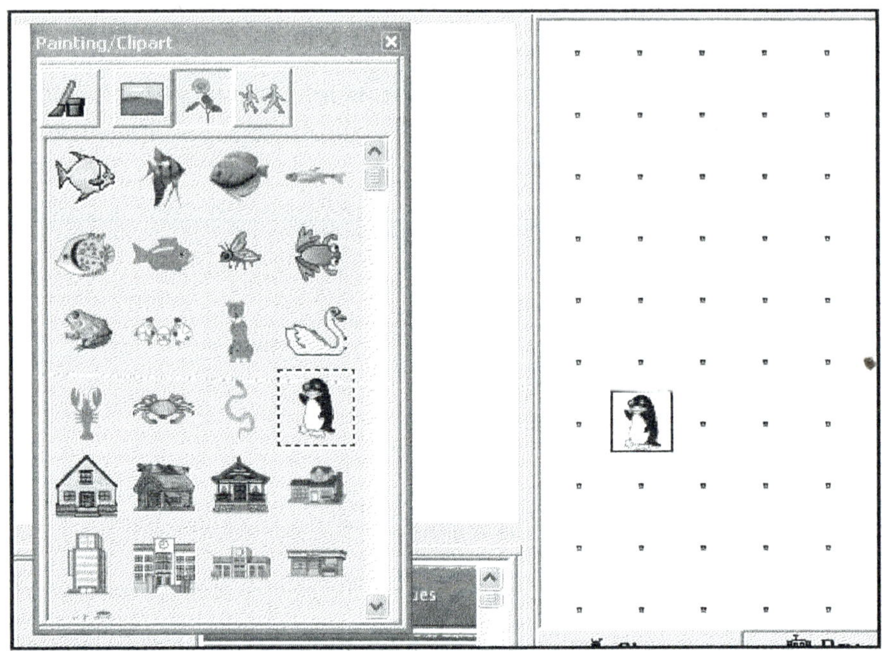

Drag individual shapes from the drawing/painting window to the shapes window to install them. When the shape is installed, pause your mouse over it to see its name, number, and size in pixels. Once a shape is installed in this way, you can use it in your programs. For a running horse, you will need to install and use horse5, horse6, and horse7 instead of horse1, horse2, and horse3 as described in the text for MicroWorlds 2.0. For a dog, you will need doggy1 and doggy2 instead of dog1 and dog2. You will also need to substitute other shapes when you can't find the shape described in the text for MicroWorlds 2.0. Don't be discouraged; the EX shapes are very nice and more finely drawn than those in MicroWorlds 2.0!

If you are deciding between MicroWorlds 2.0 and EX, here are the advantages of each at press time:

> **2.0:** Less expensive, and the graphics area is bigger. Runs on older as well as newer computers. Available through Motherboard Books at 20 percent off retail.

> **EX**: More expensive, no need to toggle back and forth between Procedures and Graphics Pages, shapes more finely drawn. Available only through the software owner, LCSI, at www.microworlds.com. See the online ordering section and look for a single home user license "set," costing around $100, plus shipping.

Part 1: MicroWorlds Games

#1 Review of Procedures, Input, and Variables

What Will I Learn?

We are building on what we learned in *Computer Science Pure and Simple Book 1*. At first, we will review a little bit, just to get the key concepts back into our heads.

What Is a Program?

A program is *a list of instructions to the computer*. Let's suppose we are going to give someone a list of simple instructions in English on how to set the table. This list of instructions might look like this:

> **get a plate from the cupboard**
> **walk to the table**
> **put it on the table**
> **return to the cupboard**
> **get a glass**
> **... and so on.**

But a set of instructions for a computer is written using a specific list of words that the computer can understand. For example, **forward 50** means "go forward 50 turtle paces." These action words for the computer, like **forward**, are *procedures*.

Instructions and Procedures

First, start with an instruction.

In the Command Center (the area at the bottom of the screen) type **cc** (stands for clear the Command Center) and press **Enter** to execute the command. Then type the following line:

> **pd forward 50 right 90 forward 50 right 90 forward 50 right 90 forward 50 right 90**

When the cursor is at the very end, press **Enter**. Presto! Our first instruction causes the turtle to draw a square.

Let's analyze our one long line of instruction. All the words you see on the line are names of procedures:

> **pd:** A procedure that puts the current turtle's pen down and requires no inputs and has no outputs

> **forward:** A procedure that moves the current turtle in the direction its head is pointing, using a certain number of steps. The number is a required input.

> **right:** A procedure that turns the current turtle to the right by a number of degrees. The number is a required input.

The last two procedures require a number as their input. One very important thing to notice is that some procedures require inputs and some don't. If you're feeling confused, read on! Or, better yet, look up the more detailed explanation in *Computer Science Pure and Simple Book 1.*

Procedure Inputs and Output

Logo procedures can be thought of as jigsaw puzzle pieces, and our job as programmers is to build puzzles which fit together properly. The key to this is the concept of inputs. The procedures that we will build, and the built-in procedures that come with MicroWorlds, each have a specified number of inputs. It can be zero inputs (such as **pd**) or one input (such as **forward**) or more inputs (such as **sum**). A procedure can also have zero outputs (such as **forward**) or one output (such as **sum**).

A procedure that needs no inputs is simply a square jigsaw puzzle piece. One that needs one input has a hole on the right for a tab. The output puzzle piece next to it has a tab sticking out on the left. So they fit together. When we use procedures in an instruction, we must provide the required inputs, and we must provide a place for the outputs to go. Think of it as a one-line jigsaw puzzle.

Here are two procedures:

As you can see, **forward** has a hole that needs a number input and, of course, 50 has a number output that will fit just fine.

Procedures that expect one number as their input will have the right size opening to fit a number. In fact, a number is really a procedure with one output (the number) and no inputs.

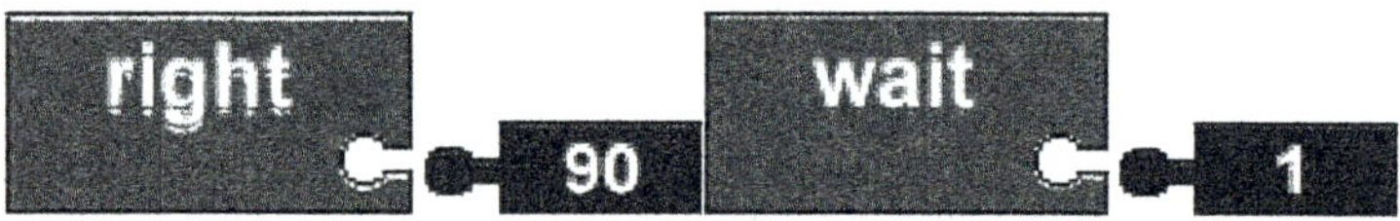

If an instruction is going to work, then all the openings and tabs must be used. Note that this means that an instruction can't begin with a procedure that has an output.

Programming with Style

A computer program has to achieve more than just doing the job. It needs to have staying power— meaning that it needs to be easily understood and changed by others. Here are some goals to keep in mind when writing a program:

1. Set up the plan of attack ahead of time.

2. Use small, one-purpose-only procedures whenever possible. This makes it easy for someone to change them later.

3. Document your work so the next person can understand it.

4. The code must work every time for everyone.

5. Choose consistent, sensible names for procedures.

Where to Write Your Program?

If you click on the MicroWorlds menu selection **Pages** and then **Procedures**, you are presented with a blank page. This Procedures Page is where as much of your code as possible belongs. You can toggle back and forth between the Procedures Page and Page1 where the turtle is drawing by pushing **ctrl** and **f** at the same time. You can also use the Pages menu and select Page1 when you want to go there. The Command Center at the bottom of Page1 is for running a procedure or an individual line of code.

Write a Procedure

Now we are going to write a set of detailed instructions for MicroWorlds to draw a square. This is the essence of programming: namely, adding new procedures and capabilities to the existing ones that came with the language.

What shall we call our new word? How about **square**? Then, when we want the turtle to move in the shape of a square, we can just type **square**, instead of that long instruction we developed above.

On the Procedures Page, type the following:

```
to square
 pd forward 50 right 90 forward 50 right 90 forward 50 right 90 forward 50 right 90
end
```

Now, go back to the Command Center on Page1 and type **square**, and then press **Enter**, to run it. Oops! It went too fast! Before we slow the movement down, there is another problem with our **square** procedure. As it is now, it is not really very readable. Let's write the same long instruction over many lines, making it much more readable. Switch to the Procedures Page and change your procedure so it looks like this:

```
to square
 pd
 forward 50 right 90
 forward 50 right 90
 forward 50 right 90
 forward 50 right 90
end
```

That is much more readable and you can see at a glance how it works. Notice that our procedure **square** takes no inputs and has no output, so its puzzle piece looks like this:

It is a "satisfied" instruction all by itself.

Now back to improving our first procedure. To slow down the movement of the turtle, let's add a built-in procedure, **wait**, after each turn that the turtle makes. **Wait** takes one input, a number.

Also, we are going to use **repeat**. **Repeat** has two inputs: the number of times to repeat an instruction, and a list of the instructions to repeat enclosed in brackets like [this].

Change your procedure so it looks like this:

```
to square
 pd
 repeat 4 [forward 50 right 90 wait 1]
end
```

Hit **Ctrl-F** to switch to Page1, and we'll give it a try! We type **square** in the Command Center. Presto, we have a square!

Now, we want to make a program using our procedure. We need a **Main** procedure and a **Start** procedure that calls **Main**. Do you remember how to make them? Add a **Start** button using the icon that looks like a finger pushing a button. (Look in the answer key in the Appendix after you have worked with it for a while, if you are stuck. Do the same with later lessons.) Remember to put double lines around the **Main** procedure, so you can find it easily. We also want to list our procedures in alphabetical order on the Procedures Page. Save this program as **Square**. You'll need it soon.

Review of Variables

What if we want to draw a building and we want to be able to tell the computer to draw it twice as big as before? Or half as big? We do this with *variables*. These are values, like the height of the building, that can vary, or change, but at the same time are represented with just one name. *Height* is an example of a variable name.

When you start a program, such as MicroWorlds or Word or Excel, you usually double click on an icon. This is an instruction to the operating system to look on the hard drive and find the program that is associated with the icon. When the operating system finds it, the operating system reads it into working memory (also called loading it) and executes or "runs" the program. This is why, in the PC world, files that run usually end with ".exe" for execute. Working memory is the place where programs are temporarily stored and where they live as they are running. This is the RAM (read-only memory) that you buy when you buy your computer. In it there are millions of places, each with an address, where the program, and we as programmers, can store things.

Pigeonhole Mailbox Named Gus

Imagine that the working memory contains a bunch of pigeonholes, like mailboxes in a post office. To use one of these storage places, we need to reserve the spot and name it. Let's pick one and give it a name—how about "Gus" ? Then we can use Gus to hold a number, word, or list. Suppose we want to use or change what's in the mailbox. Since we have named the mailbox, we can tell the computer where to find it.

So, how do we go about reserving and naming the storage spot? MicroWorlds has some built-in procedures and operators to assist us.

local reserves and names a storage place.

make puts a value in it.

":" allows us to grab what's in the variable for us to use. We read **:stepSize** as "what's in stepSize," for example.

Let's set up a test program to investigate using **local, make**, and **":"**.

Test program

Open MicroWorlds, and then open a new project.

Now we will make a little procedure to use to experiment with variables. We'll call our first variable **Var1**. We want to reserve and name our variable (storage place) using **local,** and then we want to print what's in the storage place using **show.** We also want to put in comments, marked by a semicolon ";" to remind us what we are doing. Remember to use a " sign before a word that isn't a procedure; it's like telling Logo it will be looking at a noun rather than a verb.

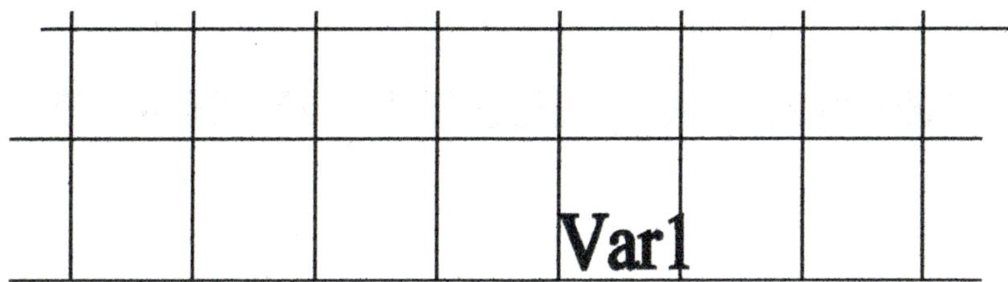

Mailbox Named Var1

Write the following procedure on the Procedures Page:

```
to TestVar
  local "Var1 ;reserves and names a storage place
  show "Var1 ;we want to print the value in the storage place
end
```

Remember that anything on the same line right after a semicolon ";" is not read by the computer, and we use this symbol before we write a comment addressed to human beings who are reading our code.

Let's call **TestVar** from **Main** by editing **Main** to be

```
==============
to Main
  TestVar
end
==============
```

(Remember, **Main** has double lines around it.) As always, it helps to view the jigsaw puzzles:

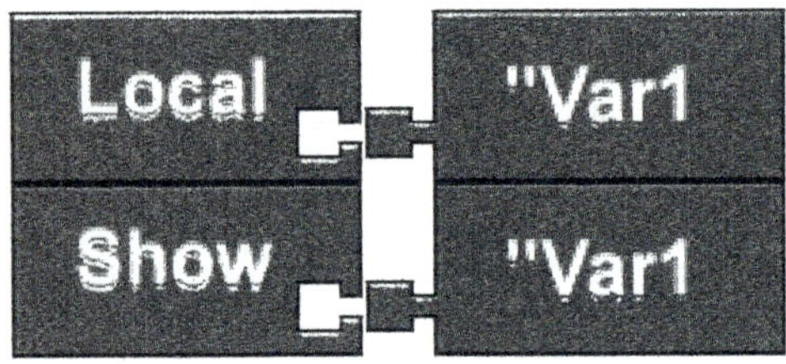

You'll also need a **Start** button and a **Start** procedure:

```
Start
  Main
end
```

Now go back to the Graphics Page, **Page1**, and click on the **Start** button. You will see:

Oops! We didn't expect this. This is the name of the variable (a mailbox name), not what is in the variable (a number).

The built-in procedure **local** is a procedure with one input and no outputs. It tells MicroWorlds to reserve a mailbox in memory to store things in, and it tells MicroWorlds that we will name this mailbox **Var1**.

Show is a very handy procedure that takes one input (a word or a list) and prints it on the Command Center. It is a good procedure to use for experimenting.

I want to know what the value is inside the mailbox named Var1. The line, **show "Var1**, is an instruction to put the word Var1 on the Command Center. This is not really what I meant!

MicroWorlds Logo uses a colon, "**:**", as an operator to indicate the *value* stored in the memory spot. So we will say **show :Var1,** meaning *show what's in Var1*.

Change your **TestVar** procedure as follows:

> **to TestVar**
>   **local "Var1 ; reserves and names a storage place**
>   **show :Var1 ; show what's in Var1**
> **end**

and run your program. Here is the result I get:

Oops again! We get an error message, telling us that we haven't put a value into the storage space. When we look at our procedure we can see this is true; we made a storage space (a variable) but we didn't tell MicroWorlds what to put it in it. We goofed. **It is a programming error to try to use a value from a variable if none has ever been stored there.**

We have one more procedure to learn, and then we can get into some serious variable experimenting. There is a built-in procedure **make** that does the job of storing values in previously named variables. It takes two inputs and has no outputs. The first input is the name of the variable, and the second is the value to be stored. It looks like this:

When we use it, it looks like this:

> **make "Var1 20**

Each input must be a naming word, not an action word or procedure. MicroWorlds uses a " before a naming word, so it can tell the difference. Numbers don't need the " because they are recognizable as naming words.

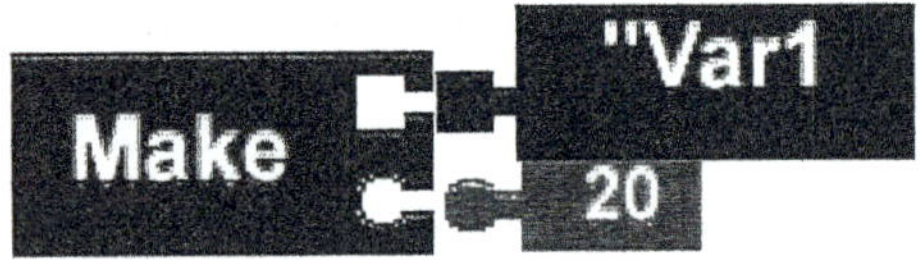

Or, using our mailbox diagram:

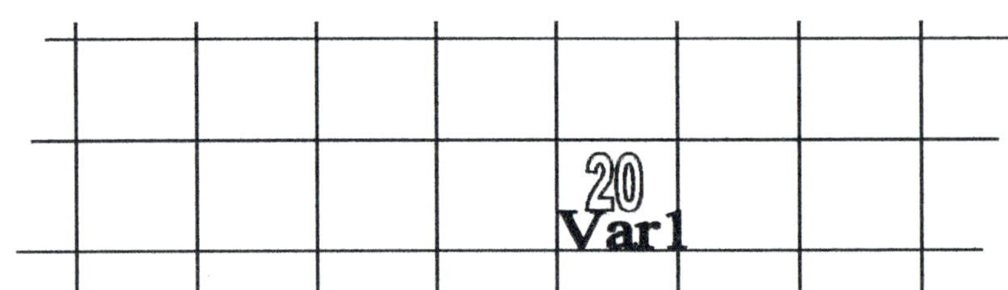

Mailbox with Contents

Change your procedure to the following:

```
to TestVar
  local "Var1 ;creates and names a variable
  make "Var1 20 ;puts the value 20 in the variable
  show :Var1 ;prints the value in the variable
end
```

We use **local** to make a variable named **Var1**.

We use **make** to put the value **20** in the variable.

We use **show** to show **:Var1**, *what's in* **Var1**.

I think it should all work this time! Before you run your program, so that your Command Center shows only the newest messages, add the **cc** instruction (clear Command Center) in **Main**, like this:

```
to Main
  cc
  TestVar
end
```

This of course just clears out the Command Center as you start your program each time. Now run your program.

Bingo! The value stored is **20** ! Let's also put in **50** and see what happens.

```
to TestVar
  local "Var1
  make "Var1 20
  show :Var1 ;this means show what's in Var1
  make "Var1 50
  show :Var1
end
```

Again, using our mailbox diagram:

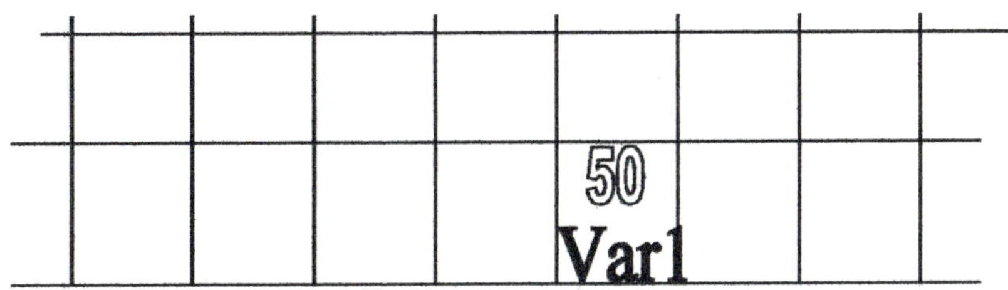

Mailbox with New Contents

We replaced the value stored, and the first one is gone forever.

If you find variables confusing, don't worry. Just work with them for a while, and they will become familiar. Proceed to the games! I will show you how to use them for real.

Exercises

1. Make the Command Center show this, using two variables, **tall** and **short:**

   60

   80

2. Now make it show this, using one variable, **tall:**

   30

   40

#2 Madlibs

We are going to work on a new project, a game called Madlibs. It will give us some more practice dealing with variables.

We are going to follow a defined set of steps in programming this. They are:

1. Decide on the goal.

2. "Sandbox" to acquire necessary knowledge

3. Write pseudocode, which describes in English what we want to do

4. Code

5. Test

6. Do it all again, that is, "enhance."

Probably you have played Madlibs before, not using a computer. You interview someone, writing down a noun, the name of a vegetable, or whatever, using the person you are talking to as a random generator. Then you put the words into a story that you have already written, that has blanks for the noun, the name of a vegetable, and so on. The result is pleasantly nonsensical, and you can both enjoy it.

To do the project, we need to follow our programming steps!

1. Decide on the goal

In this step you need to think about exactly what you want the procedure to accomplish. There are always a few little decisions to be made, and now is the time to make them.

We will capture words from the user, save them, and then plug them into a story that prints out on Page1. We will use our knowledge of variables. We want to create a variable that will capture a word typed in by the user. Then we will keep the words stored until time to use them. So we will need as many variables as there are blanks in the story. Here is our assignment:

- Make a madlib using at least five variables.

- Ask the user to give us words to put in the variables.

- Print out a story using the five variables into a text box.

- Make a procedure called **madlibs** that works with a **Main** and a **Start** procedure.

2. Sandbox to acquire necessary knowledge

This step is a *learning* step. Here you look at your goal and see if there are some aspects that you need to learn more about before you can write the code. If so, then you write some "sandbox" or "throw-away" code to teach yourself what you need to know.

We need to know how to accept words typed in by the user. Here is an example. Suppose we create and name a variable called **noun1**. Open a new file. On your Procedures Page, start a new procedure called **Madlibstest**. Then add a line to create a variable, **noun1**:

> **to madlibstest**
> **local "noun1**

Here's what we have created:

Mailbox with Unknown Contents Called Noun1

Now we type in this code:

> **question [What is your favorite animal?]**

This procedure, **question**, asks the user a question and gives space for an answer.

> **make "noun1 answer**

The procedure **answer** outputs whatever the user just typed. The procedure **make** gives the variable **noun1** the value of answer. Let's say the user typed "worm." At this point, the variable **noun1** would contain "worm."

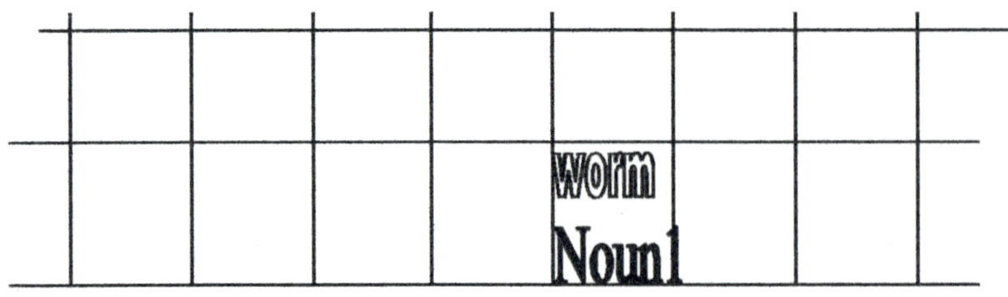

Mailbox with New Contents

Let's see what's going on. Your preliminary procedure looks like this:

```
to madlibstest
  local "noun1
  question [Please type in an animal name.]
  make "noun1 answer
  show :noun1 ;this means show what's in noun1
end
```

Go to the Command Center and type **madlibstest,** to run the procedure. Type in an animal name as requested. Does the computer show the animal name at the bottom of the screen? It is supposed to.

But let's make a text box and print our output in that. That way, we can use our game without using the Command Center. We would need that if we posted it on the Web. To make a text box, go to Page1. Click the icon box with ABC in it. Then click on the screen and size your text box to make it at least half the size of the screen. You can right click on the text box and tell it to hide the box name.

To print into the text box, we use the command **print**, instead of **show** for the Command Center.

The MicroWorlds **Help** button index tells us this about **print**:

print

print (pr) word-or-list

Prints a word or list in the current text box. The text is followed by a carriage return and line feed sequence. See insert.

Example:

repeat 5 [print "hello]

The suggested format is **print word-or-list**. A *word* has a " mark right before it. A *list* is enclosed in [brackets]. So our input needs to have one or the other, " mark or brackets. Try these in the Command Center:

print "hello

print [hello]

print [[hello] [Mom]]

Can you get it to print "Hello out there!" ? Try it before you turn the page.

Our "Hello out there!" would look like this:

print [Hello out there!]

How do we get it to print out **what's in (:)** a variable? On the Procedures Page, let's try this:

to test
  local "noun1
  make "noun1 "me
  print [Hello :noun1]
end

Type **test** in the Command Center, and press **Enter.** Oops!! It printed "Hello :noun1" in the text box! That's not what we want! We want *what's in* **noun1!**

Let's look at a procedure called **sentence**. Here's what Help has to say about **sentence**:

sentence (se) word-or-list1 word-or-list2

(sentence word-or-list1 word-or-list2 word-or-list3...)

Reports a list which is made up of its inputs (words or lists). Sentence can take more than 2 inputs when sentence and the inputs are enclosed in parentheses. See list.

Examples:

show sentence "a "b

a b

show (sentence "hi "there [Bill])

hi there Bill

This is telling us to use this format:

print (sentence input1 input2 input3)

Notice the parentheses that include the word **sentence** and all the inputs. Each of these inputs needs to be one of these:

1. a word, with a " mark

2. a list, using [brackets]

3. "what's in" a variable, for example **:noun1**.

I want you to look at these commands, and guess which ones should work. Then test them in a test procedure. To make them work, first type this into the procedure:

```
to test
 local [animal age]
 make "animal "cow
 make "age 13
 ;put test sentence here
end
```

To test each one, make sure you have a text box. Then type **test** in the Command Center to run the **test** procedure. You don't have to keep typing **test**; just put the cursor right after the word and press **Enter**. That will run it too. Here are your test sentences:

```
print (sentence "the :animal "ran)
print (sentence [The very large] :animal [ran through the woods])
print [Hello there] [How are you?]
print sentence [Hello there][How are you?}
print (sentence [Hello there] [How are you] [today?])
print (sentence [My age is ] :age [years.])
```

For grins, change the animal and the age in the variables and run them again. You could make a very large mouse run through the woods!

Now that we know more on this subject, let's get interactive and collect those variable contents from the user. In our **madlibstest** procedure on the Procedures Page, add these underlined lines:

```
To madlibstest
  local "noun1
  question [Please type in an animal name.]
  make "noun1 answer
  show :noun1
  print (sentence "hello "there :noun1)
  print (sentence [What are we talking about?] :noun1)
end
```

Now go to the Command Center and type **madlibstest.** Press **Enter.**

What do you get? Do some more experimenting.

We're well on our way to making a madlib!

Now, what if we want to create several variables at once? We'll need at least five variables. Let's guess that **local** might be able to help us. Look up **local** under the Help index. It says this:

local

local word-or-list

So we can use either a single word (with quote mark) or a list (with square brackets) as an input for local. For instance, we can say:

local "fred

for one variable, or for several:

local [fred sam bob]

We need a list because we want to create five variables. Let's try this at the top of the **madlibstest** procedure:

local [noun1 noun2 noun3 noun4 adj1 adv1]

In fact, it is standard procedure in programming to create your variables at the top of the procedure, and then do the rest of the coding. So let's plan to do that.

We need one more procedure that allows us to talk to the user. Let's try **announce**. The Help menu tells us this:

announce

announce word-or-list

Displays the message in an alert box. Clicking OK closes the box. See **question** *and* **answer**.

So the input for **announce** can be a list of words in brackets. Let's test this in the Command Center:

announce [Here is your madlib.]

Does it work? Let's add these ideas to our **madlibstest**. We can use these new tools: **question, print, sentence, local** using a list of variables, and **announce**.

```
To madlibstest
  local [noun1 noun2 verb3 adj4 noun5]
  question [Please type in an animal name.]
  make "noun1 answer
  announce [Here is your madlib.]
  print (sentence [One day the] :noun1 [took a walk in the rain.])
end
```

Planning

The next thing you need to do for our **madlibs** procedure is to write a simple story on a piece of paper or in a word processor. Underline five words that you will be erasing, but don't choose verbs (action words). Verbs are too hard to get right when asking input from the user. Separately, write down a question for each word. (Remember, the question needs to ask the user for a word of the same type, not exactly the same word, or the madlib won't end up being funny.) Keep the questions in order. Next to each question, write down a good variable name for that underlined word, for example, noun1, noun2, noun3, adj1, adv1, and so on.

3. Pseudocode

Pseudocode is just like program code except that it is written in English. It helps us make a quick and easy plan without worrying yet about getting details exactly right.

Go to the Procedures Page and type **to madlibs**, to begin your pseudocode. Put a semicolon at the beginning of the next line so we know it is pseudocode. First make pseudocode for creating and naming your variables. For example:

> **to madlibs**
> **;create and name variables noun1, noun2, noun3, noun4, adj1, adv1**

Your second line of pseudocode will ask the user a relevant question for the first missing word, such as "Please describe a feeling" or "Give me an adverb, such as slowly, quickly, heavily, etc." Write that pseudocode, with semicolon. For example:

> **;ask the user to type an animal name**

Your third line of pseudocode will take the word from the user and store it in the first variable. For example,

> **;store the animal name in a variable named noun1.**

Do the same for the next variable and the next until you have five variables. Write these lines of pseudocode.

Your next line of pseudocode will announce "Here is your madlib." Write this.

Finally we have the story-writing section. Write pseudocode lines for printing out your story into the text box, inserting the right variables in the right places. For example:

> **;print "There once was a noun1. One day the noun1 went to the park and saw a noun2."**

Now, show your teacher. Your teacher can compare it with the pseudocode in the answer key and give you pointers.

4. Code

Translate your pseudocode into code, that is, into Logo. In other words, after each line of pseudocode with a **;** in front of it, put a real line of code that says the same thing in Logo. Your code should be based on our latest version of **madlibstest**. Look at **madlibstest** to figure out how to translate each line of pseudocode into code.

5. Test

Test your creation by typing **madlibs** in the Command Center. Then make a **Main** procedure that calls **madlibs** and a **Start** procedure that calls **Main.** Make a **Start** button. Does it work? Now you have a complete program. Check with the answers in the back of the book if you are having trouble.

Exercise

Make a second Madlib with a different story and different variables, totaling 7 variables instead of 5.

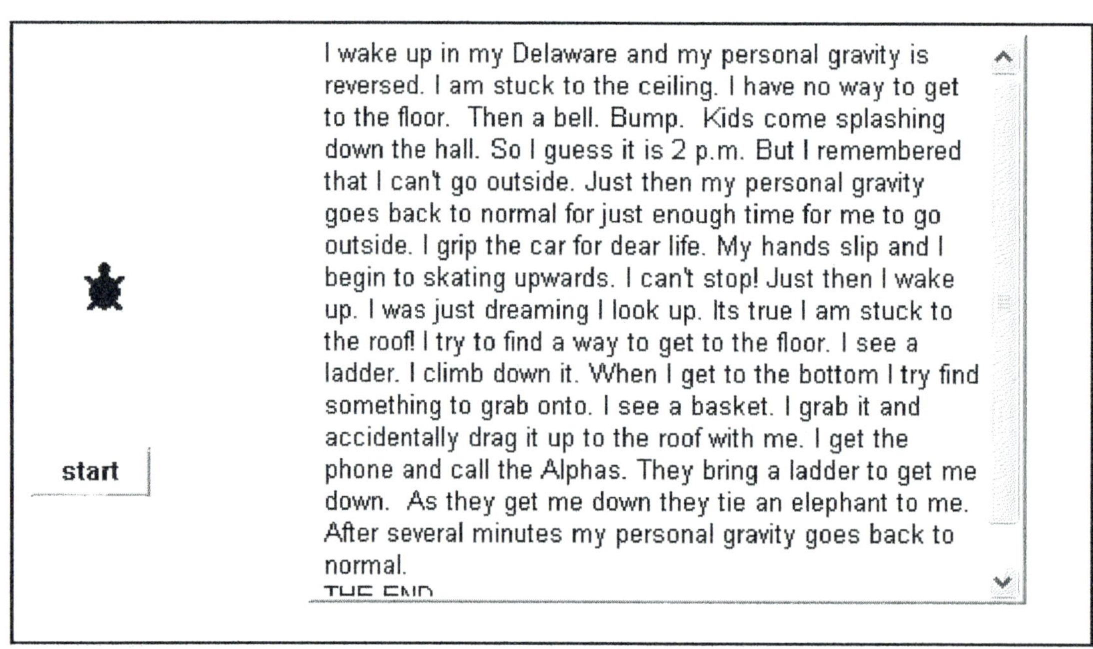

Stephen's Madlib Results

#3 Madlibs II

Let's work on it some more!

Decide on the Goal

Now we want to add another procedure; we'll call it **intro**. It chats with the user a little and then asks whether the user wants to play madlibs. This way, we'll get some practice with the **if-then statement**, another element that is common to all computer languages.

Here's the pseudocode for it:

```
to intro
;makes a dialogue box to ask "What's your name?"
;says, "I like your name."
;asks, "Would you like to play madlibs? Y or N"
;if the user answers Y, then go to madlibs
;otherwise, say "Bye!"
end
```

Sandbox to Acquire Necessary Knowledge

We need to learn about if-then statements. We want to do one thing if the user answers Y, and something else if the user answers anything else.

Let's consider this statement:

If it is raining, then you need to take your umbrella.

The first part is a condition which we need to test. Is it true or not true? If it is true, then we take the action following, namely take the umbrella.

This is a type of statement that a computer can understand. We can write

if (it is raining) [take your umbrella]

The (it is raining) condition has what is called a **Boolean** value: it is either true or false. (This is named after an English mathematician, George Boole.)

This type of situation where there are only two alternatives is very easily understood by a computer, which is really just a bunch of on-off switches (or T-F switches). So as the computer reads the condition, it will evaluate and assign a T or an F value to it. If the condition is true, it will execute the action. If it isn't true, it just goes on down to the next line.

Now, a computer inside a building might have some trouble figuring out whether it is raining. It would need to read sensors on the outside of the building. But there are many problems it can easily evaluate to T or F. For example, it can ask the user for a number, and it can test the number to see whether it is greater than 1.

Or it can ask the user for a letter, and test to see if the letter is a Y. In the case of our problem at hand here, we can type,

If (answer = "y)
  [madlibs]

Pseudocode

I gave you some pseudocode already. Here it is again:

to intro
; makes a dialogue box to ask "What's your name?"
; says, "I like your name."
; asks, "Would you like to play Madlibs? Y or N"
; if the user answers Y, then go to Madlibs
;say "Bye!"
end

Code

Let's make that into code.

Change **Main** so that it calls **intro** instead of **madlibs**. You're calling **madlibs** now from **intro**, not from **Main.**

Test

Now let's test it. First, let's put it into presentation mode. On the top of the Page1 screen is a series of menus. Select **Gadgets**, and under it, **Presentation Mode**. (In MicroWorlds EX, this is under the **View** menu.) Your screen changes. (To get out of **Presentation Mode**, click on the black area around the screen.) Push the **Start** button and run through the madlib.

What happens if the computer asks if you want to play madlibs, and you type something besides Y? The computer goes on to the next line of code. Also, what happens after you go through your madlib and finish it? If you followed this pseudocode, you'll soon get the same thing both times: the computer tells you "Bye!"

But this isn't quite what I want. I want it to say "Bye!" only if the user types something besides Y and refuses to play. So it needs more work.

Do it again

We need to sandbox some more. We want the computer to do one thing (play madlibs) if the answer is Y, and something else (say "Bye!") if the answer is other than Y. In most computer languages this is called an **If-then-else** statement. We would be writing something like this:

> **If (answer equals Y) go to madlibs**
> **else**
> **print "Bye!"**

After the **else** is the secondary command, which is executed if the condition (answer equals Y) is false. **Else** is a shorthand way of saying "otherwise." This is the way it is in several other computer languages.

But in Logo, the if-then-else sequence is a bit nonstandard. Let's review: Logo has a procedure called **if** that has two inputs. One is the condition, evaluating to true or false. The other is the command to execute if the value is true.

> **if (condition) [command to execute if true]**

If we look in the Help menu, we see that Logo also has a procedure called **ifelse** that has three inputs: the condition for evaluation to true or false, the command to execute if the value is true, and the command to execute if the value is false.

> **ifelse (condition) [command to execute if true] [command to execute if false]**

Exercises

1. Use **ifelse** in your code and modify your game so that it follows this pseudocode:

> **;If (answer equals Y) go to madlibs, otherwise print "Bye!"**

2. Invent a game called One Question (a very dumb version of Twenty Questions). Use these instructions to write your pseudocode (lines of instruction in English that start with a semicolon, or ";"). You will need a **Start** button and a text box. You need procedures for **Start**, **Main**, **intro**, and **oneq**. **Start** calls **Main**. **Main** calls **intro**.

A procedure called **intro** asks the user's name and says it likes it. It asks if the user wants to play One Question. If the answer is Y, the computer calls the procedure **oneq**. If it is not Y, it says "Bye!"

The procedure **oneq** has a local variable, **quiznumber**. The procedure puts the number 4 in that variable. Then the computer asks the user to guess a number between 0 and 10. The computer compares the stored number to the guess. If the answer is greater than what's in **quiznumber**, the computer announces "too big!" If the answer is smaller than what's in **quiznumber**, it announces "too small!" If the answer equals what's in **quiznumber**, it announces "You got it!" Then it prints a sentence reporting the number stored in **quiznumber**.

Construct your pseudocode from the instructions, putting semicolons before each line. Then after each pseudocode line, write a line of code in Logo without the semicolon. Test it and get it to work. Change the 4 stored in **quiznumber** to something else. Get a friend to play your game.

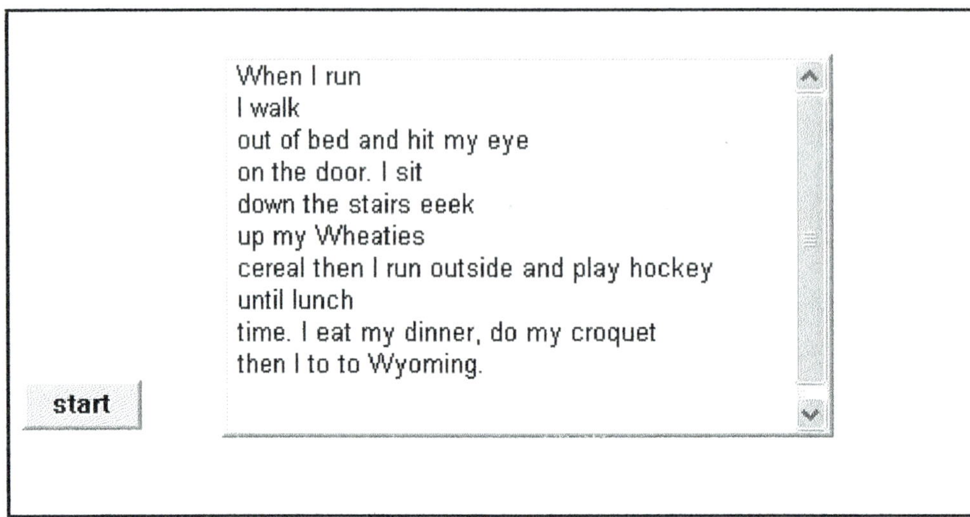

Lianna's Madlib

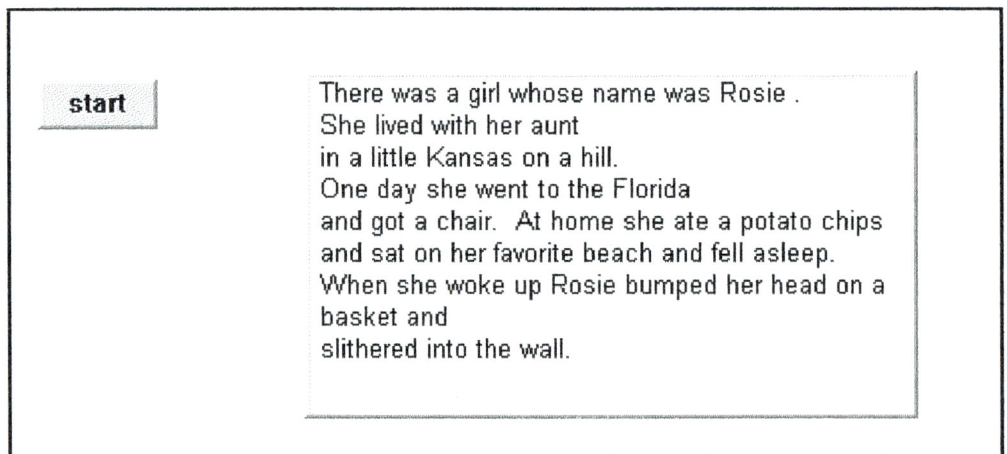

Elisa's Madlib

#4 Review of Animation Using Variables

Pull up your **Square** file, or type in the following:

```
to Main

end
```

```
to square
  repeat 4 [forward 50 right 90 wait 1]
end

to Start
  Main
end
```

Now it's time to add an action figure. I want you to add some lines to Main so it looks like this:

```
to Main
  cc
  talkto "t1
  setsh [horse1 horse2 horse3]
  repeat 20 [square]
end
```

This is a simple animation. Hopefully you recognize a list of turtle shapes using **setsh** for set shape. Now, every time the computer calls **forward**, it goes back to the shape list and picks the next shape. We have chosen shapes that similar, but the legs are in different positions. Our **square** procedure contains calls to **forward**, and **square** is repeated, so the computer keeps coming to **forward** commands inside **square** and changing the shape according to the list. The result looks like a horse running. The shapes can be shapes already given in MicroWorlds, or we can make them by clicking on a blank in the Shapes Center and using drawing tools.

Adding an Input to Our Procedure

It would be nice if we could decide how big a square our turtle should make. Then we would have a nice, general procedure that could be used anytime we want a square of any size. You won't believe how easy it is to make this improvement, now that we understand variables.

We want to turn our procedure **square,** which currently has no inputs and no outputs, into a procedure that receives one input. We do that simply by thinking of a good name for the storage spot for the input—how about length?—and putting it on the line that declares the procedure. We will use **what's in length,** written **:length.** Make the following change to **square:**

```
to square :length
  repeat 4 [forward 50 right 90 wait 1]
end
```

We just used a shortcut! Instead of using the instruction **local,** we put the new variable name in the first line of the procedure. This takes a spot in memory and names it **length** so we can store a value in it.

Again, using our mailbox diagram, we can see our variable.

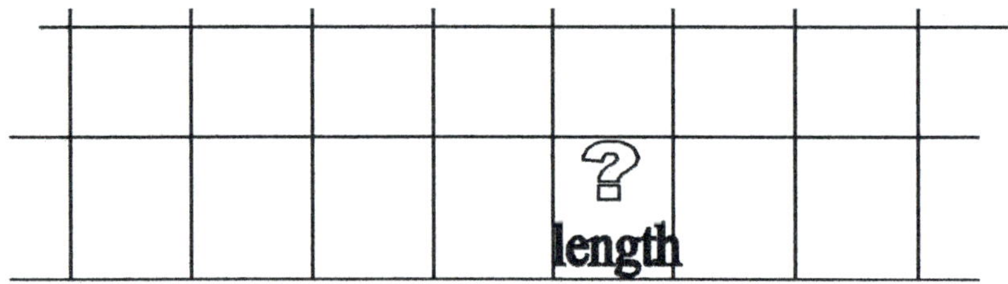

Mailbox with Unknown Contents

The neat thing is that we don't have to use **make** to put the value in. We pass the value to the **square** procedure when we call it. In other words, when we use the **square** procedure, we need to place an input next to it that will go into the mailbox. The code in **Main** needs to say, for example,

square 30

instead of just **square.**

When the computer gets to **square 30,** right at that point, a 30 goes into the mailbox named **length** and waits to be used by the procedure **square.**

So **square** now needs one input. Its jigsaw piece looks like this now:

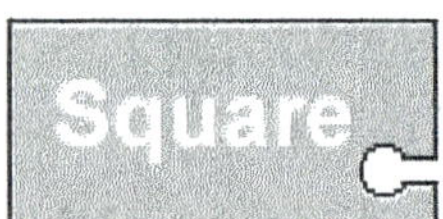

Now we need to change **Main.** Instead of typing **square,** we will type **square 30.**

```
to Main
  cc
  talkto "t1
  setsh [horse1 horse2 horse3]
  repeat 20 [square 30]
end
```

Now you can try your program, and you will find that it works, but it really isn't any better than before. Our revised procedure **square** requires an input and gets an input, but it doesn't actually use it for anything!

Let's fix **square** so that it makes use of the variable **length.** We want the value stored in **length** to be used as the input to **forward.** Do you remember how? Take a minute to think about it.

Instead of saying **forward 50**, we'll say **forward what's in length**. Instead of "what's in," use a colon before the variable name. Change your **square** procedure as follows:

```
to square :length
  repeat 4
    [forward :length right 90 wait 1]
end
```

Now, to find the input for **forward,** Logo must find the value stored in **length.** Where did that value come from? The value is stored there when Main calls the procedure **square** using a number.

Play with your new, more powerful **square** by changing this calling value, currently **30**. Officially this value is called an *argument*. (I don't know why. I'm not mad; are you mad?) Inside the procedure the variable is called a *parameter*.

You can also call **square** directly from the Command Center, for example by typing **square 200** and pressing **Enter.**

We have now finished a very good procedure that we can use any time we want. Here is my finished program, complete with lines setting off Main from the rest of the program, and procedures in alphabetical order:

```
==============
to Main
  cc
  talkto "t1
  setsh [horse1 horse2 horse3]
  repeat 20 [square 30]
end
==============
to square :length
  repeat 4
    [forward :length right 90 wait 1]
end

to Start
  Main
end
```

Exercises

1. Test it! Put in different values for the line in **Main** that calls **square**. Use **square 40** and **square 60**.

2: Take the One Question guessing game you created in the previous lesson. Have the turtle do a little dance when someone wins.

Here's the pseudocode to add to your **oneq** procedure:

;if answer equals what's in quiznumber, do a jig

You need to write a jig procedure. Use this pseudocode:

;announce that you got the right answer
;talk to Turtle t1(talkto "t1)
;put your pen down, pd (or pen up, pu)
;repeat a number of times a list of commands that includes forward, right, etc.

After each line of pseudocode, write a line of real code in Logo without the semicolon that does the same thing. Test your creation. If it doesn't work after you have worked on it for half an hour, look at the answers in the back of the book.

Stephen drew these shapes in the Shape Center for animations of characters from Veggie Tales.

#5 The Wandering Turtle

Programming Technique

Our next project is to build a procedure that makes the turtle wander around aimlessly.

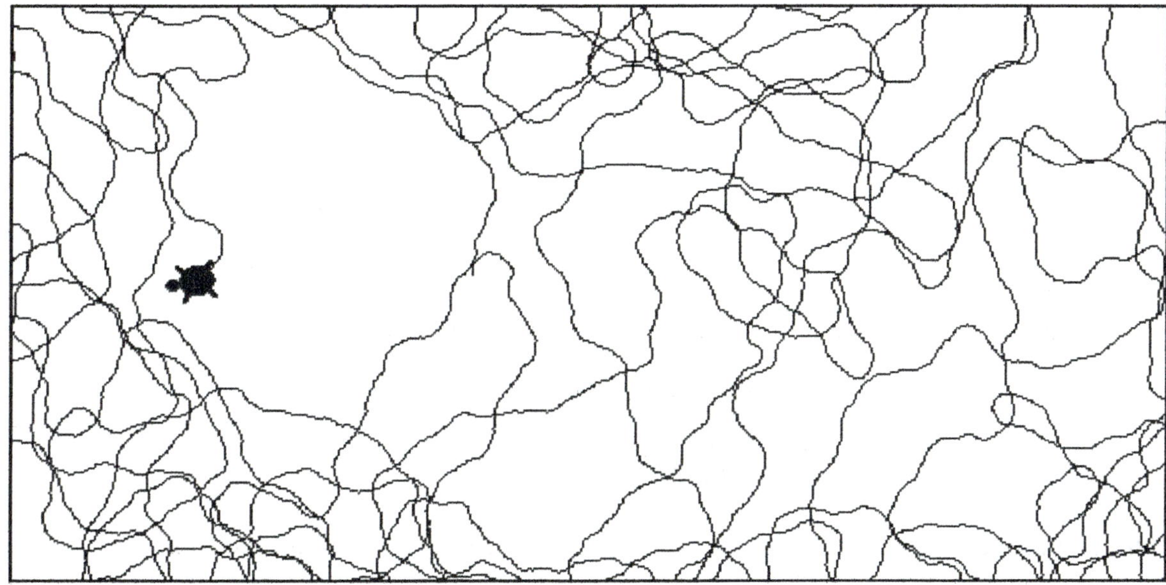

Decide on the Goal

We want our turtle to wander aimlessly. Let's have the procedure handle just one step in the turtle's aimless wander, and be called repeatedly. The procedure would slightly change the direction the turtle is going and then take one step in that direction. (Can you think of different plans for doing this?)

Sandbox to Acquire Necessary Knowledge

In our case, we want the turtle to change its direction some random amount. We will tell it to go right or left by this random amount. Random means "unpredictable." We need to learn more about this, so let's test some ideas, or sandbox.

In MicroWorlds, let's start a new project and add our usual **Start** button and code, like this:

```
to Main

end

to Start
  Main
end
```

Go to the Help screen and look up **random**.

random

*random **number***

Reports a random non-negative integer less than number.

Example:

show random 100

22

This procedure will simulate the roll of a die:

to die

show 1 + random 6

end

Random is a procedure that has one input, a number, and one output, also a number.

Random 100 generates a random number less than 100. Let's investigate. Write the following code:

```
to Main
  wander
end

to Start
  Main
end

to wander
  show random 100
end
```

Click on the **Start** button several times. We see random numbers, all less than 100, displayed in the Control Center.

In our **wander** procedure, we will want to change the direction of the turtle by a negative amount or a positive amount. **Random,** however, only outputs positive numbers. How can we make **random** give us numbers that are less than zero? Think about that one for a minute. Hint: we'll need to do some subtracting.

We need to do a little more sandboxing because we need some experience subtracting one number from another. A look in the MicroWorlds Help index turns up **difference. Difference** is a lot like **sum.**

It requires two inputs and has one output. Its output is the result of subtracting the second input from the first input. Here is what the puzzle piece looks like.

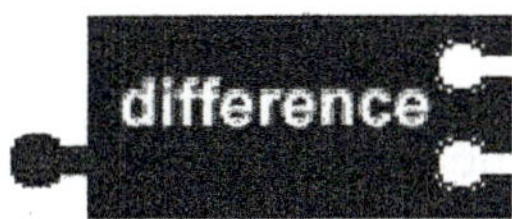

Let's sandbox with **difference**. Change your code to the following:

```
to wander
 ;show random 100
 show difference 25 10
end
```

Notice that we put a **";"** in front of the second line; this makes it a comment, not read by the computer. This is called "commenting out" some code. Try different numbers as inputs for **difference** until you are sure you understand **difference.**

Now, can you figure out how to make our procedure come up with random numbers, *half of which are less than zero?* (Hint: Use **difference** to subtract something from **random 100,** the random number less than 100.)

Don't turn the page until you think about it and try five solutions in the Command Center, using **show**. Here's how it will look, with the _ under the number you will supply:

show difference random 100 __

Here's a solution: **show difference random 100 50.** Fifty is half of 100.

We give **random** a number as input, 100. **Random** gives us an output number, say 76. We then subtract <u>half the input number of 100</u> from the 76. Seventy-six minus 50 is 26, the number that will print out.

If the number **random** puts out is less than 50, for example 30, then the number that prints out is 30 minus 50 equals –20, a negative number. So about half the time, we should be getting a negative number.

Here's the code for this solution:

```
to wander
  show difference random 100 50
end
```

Do you have difficulty figuring out that line? When you "walk through" it, starting at the left, it is a bit easier. Just be sure to think of the outputs and inputs.

show - takes one input

difference - has one output; good, **show** needs that; takes two inputs

random - has one output; good, that is one of the two needed by **difference**; needs one input

100 - has one output; good, that is the one needed by **random,** so now **random** is happy

50 - has one output; good. That is the other of the two needed by **difference,** so now **difference** is happy and it makes **show** happy .

In other words, we are subtracting **50** from the output of **random 100**, and we are showing the result.

We'll be changing our turtle's heading. There are several ways to do this, but here's a simple one: how about a right turn? Let's look at the procedure **right:**

right

right (rt) number

Turns the turtle to the right.

Example:

pd repeat 10 [fd 40 bk 20 rt 36]

If **right** has a positive input, the turtle turns to the right. If it has a negative input, the turtle turns to the left. So, half the time we will have a negative number, and so half the time the turtle will be turning left.

Write Pseudocode

Now that we have acquired some necessary knowledge, it is time to write this up as pseudocode. Here is what I want for the **wander** procedure:

to wander
;change the turtle's heading by a random amount
;move forward a certain amount twice (so the shape changes)
end

Pseudocode does not have to go into great detail, but it should be clear. In pseudocode, try not to use real names of procedures or numbers. Pseudocode also makes good comments to keep in your real code so you, or anyone else, can see at a glance what the procedure does. That's why I put a semicolon, ";", in front of it to show that it isn't real code. Typically, you would write the pseudocode sort of quick and rough as we just did and then revise it so it gets closer and closer to real code.

First, let's create and name a variable, **stepSize**, that will store the distance the turtle moves forward.

to wander :stepSize

So when we call **wander** in **Main**, we use **wander 5** to give it an input number, 5, that is stored away. Then the computer sends the 5 to the variable **stepSize** in **wander**.

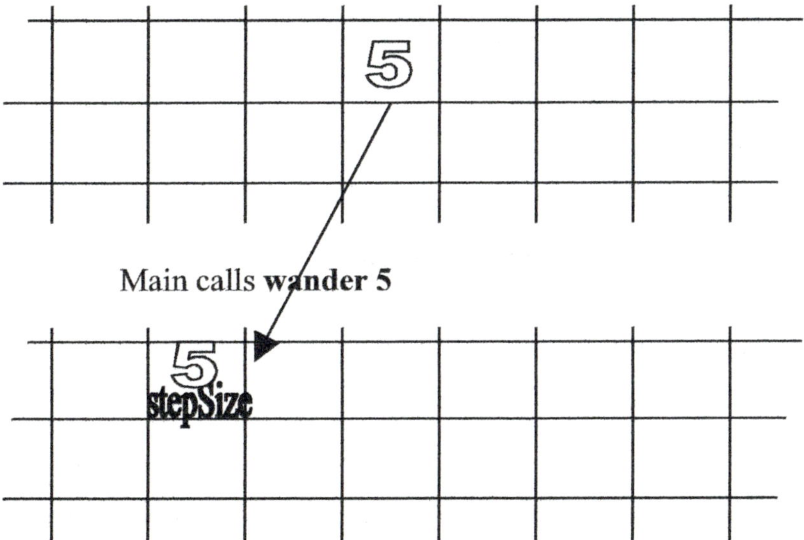

In **wander**, **wander :stepSize** stores the 5 in **stepSize**

to wander :stepSize
;change the turtle's heading by a random amount
;move forward by stepSize, twice so the shape changes
end

There, that should be close enough that we can easily code it. Now let's move on to the fun part.

Code

Now, just do what our pseudocode tells us to do.

```
to wander :stepSize
  ;change the turtle's heading by a random amount

  _______________________________________

  ;move forward by stepSize, twice so the shape changes

  _______________________________________
end
```

We want to add lines to fill in the blank lines. (You don't need to type the blank lines in your Procedures Page.)

First, let's rewrite our pseudocode making it a little more specific. We are going to use a right turn.

```
to wander :stepSize
  ;turn right by a random amount which could be negative

  _______________________________________

  ;move forward by stepSize, twice so the shape changes

  _______________________________________
end
```

We'll add a line of code and underline it so we can see it.

```
to wander :stepSize
  ;turn right by a random amount which could be negative
  right random 100
  ;move forward by stepSize, repeat twice

  _______________________________________
end
```

This is a stab at the idea we were working on before. Now, let's try it. To test our procedure, type this line into the Command Center:

```
wander 5
```

Press **Enter.** What happens? Keep doing it. The turtle keeps turning—but always to the right! Hmm, what can we do about that? We forgot to subtract something from **random 100**, to make the result negative half the time. Do you remember what to subtract? Think about it before you turn the page.

We will subtract 50 from **random 100**. Let's go over it again, in case we didn't digest it too well the first time. If **random 100** is 99, then 99 minus 50 is 49. If **random 100** is 49, then 49 minus 50 is –1. If **random 100** is 2, then 2 minus 50 is –48. So, about half the time we would get a negative number, and the turtle would be turning left instead of right. Remember?

Now, how do we encode that? We started with this:

We will have to use the procedure **difference**. What we want is the difference between random 100 and 50, or

> **difference random 100 50**

so our line of code turns into this:

> **right difference random 100 50**

Now, copy and paste this line from the Command Center to your Procedures Page, right after its pseudocode. I will underline it because it is new:

> **to wander :stepSize**
>   **;turn right by a random amount which could be negative**
> <u>**right difference random 100 50**</u>
>   **;move forward by stepSize, repeat twice**
>
> ______________________________
>
> **end**

In the Command Center, type **wander 5** to test **wander**. Keep doing it. Does it turn right sometimes and left sometimes?

Now, let's finish it. Here's the next piece of pseudocode we are looking at translating:

> **;move forward by stepSize, twice**

Can you make a line of real code that does that? Use **:stepSize** for *what's in stepSize*. Don't look while you think about it. It's exercise for your brain, stretching it like this. Again, test your line of code by typing **wander 5** in the Command Center and seeing if the turtle does what you intended.

Test

Step 4 and 5, coding and testing, are usually all mixed together. You tend to code and test, fix and test several times in the development of a procedure. Now go to your program page and click on **Start.** We get an error message! Oops! We forgot to fix our call to **wander** from **Main**! Here is a revised **Main:**

```
to Main
  repeat 60
    [wander 5]
end
```

Now test it. Oops again! Our turtle is moving too fast! We forgot the **wait.** Here is a revised **wander:**

```
to wander :stepSize
  ;turn right by a random amount which could be negative
  right difference random 100 50
  ;move forward by stepSize, repeat twice
  repeat 2 [forward :stepSize wait 1]
end
```

Try it. Neat!

Exercises

1. Adjust the **stepSize**. Test it.

2. Adjust the input to make smoother lines. How do you do that? How do you need to adjust the number subtracted from the random number? Test it.

3. Put the pen down in **Main**. (Start **Main** with **pd** for pen down).

4. Make the turtle's shape change as it wanders around. Hint: use **setsh** in **Main**.

#6 Enhanced Wandering Turtle

In the exercise for the last lesson, we adjusted the smoothness of the line the turtle is drawing. Do you remember how? We adjusted the input to random. Here's an idea: why don't we change the program so that the user can more easily make that change? Let's make the input to **random** into a variable. We can change its value by changing the number we pass to it from **Main**, just like we were doing by passing a value for **stepSize**.

Decide on the Goal—Again

Our goal before was "to <u>slightly</u> change the direction the turtle is going and then take a step in that direction." We will now enhance this goal.

New goal of **wander** : To change the direction the turtle is going, *based on a parameter to the procedure*. A parameter is a value passed to the variable. We already have one parameter, **stepSize**, passed from **Main**. We'll call our new one **dizziness**. Our call to **wander** used to be **wander 5.** Now it will be **wander 5 2,** for example. The first number goes into **stepSize** and the second number into **dizziness**.

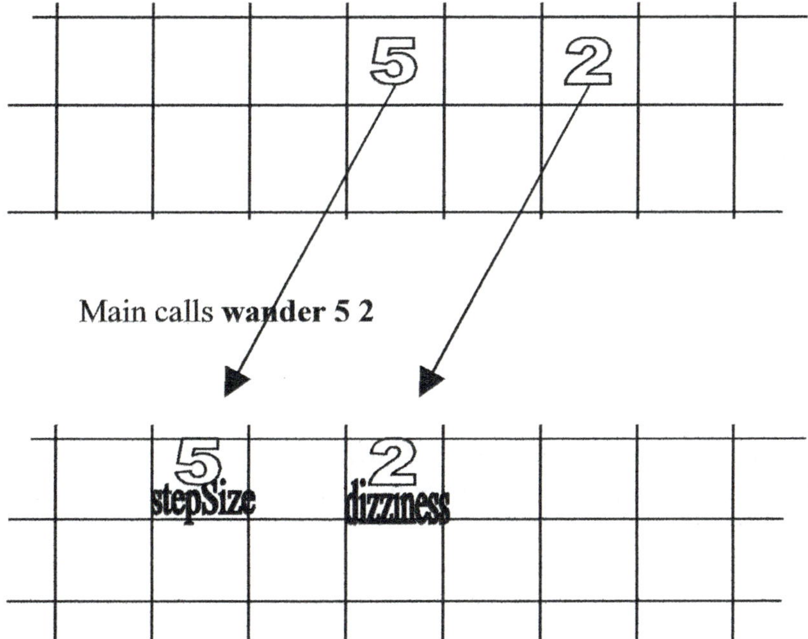

to wander :stepSize :dizziness stores the 5 in **stepSize,** and the 2 in **dizziness**.

This new variable will make **wander** more flexible. The turtle will be able to move along, more or less on track, and it will also be able to stagger around, going mostly nowhere. All we have to do is change the input numbers for **random,** which changes the input number for the **right** turn.

Sandbox to Acquire Necessary Knowledge—Again

Here is our existing **wander**:

```
to wander :stepSize
  ;turn right by a random amount which could be negative
  right difference random 100 50
  ;move forward by stepSize, repeat twice
  repeat 2 [forward :stepSize wait 1]
end
```

The number that we are going to make into a parameter instead of a "hard-coded" number is the **100** which is an input to **random.** It is this number that determines how much the heading of the turtle is changed. However, the number **50** is tied to **100**. Remember, we had to subtract **50** from the result of **random 100** so that the turtle's heading could be changed by a positive or negative amount. How did we determine the number **50**? It was half of **100**, or half of the input to **random**. So we are going to need to divide our parameter in half.

We need to know how to divide one number by another number. A quick look in the Help section shows us that **divide** is not there, but scrolling down further turns up **quotient**, as shown below. You remember from your math class that **quotient** is a fancy word for the answer to a division problem.

quotient

quotient number1 number2

Reports the result of dividing number1 by number2. See /.

Example:

show quotient 3 3

1

We have used this same type of puzzle piece before with **sum** and **difference**. To sandbox we should type in a few lines directly in the Command Center to make sure we understand how it works. Try **show quotient 80 2.** That should do it for the sandbox.

Pseudocode—Again

In the pseudocode step, let's add **dizziness** as a variable in the top line of the procedure. Let's add this second line of pseudocode as a comment. I will underline the new stuff.

```
to wander :stepSize :dizziness
  ;turn right by a random amount which could be negative
  ;turn right by a random amount up to dizziness
  right difference random 100 50
```

```
;move forward by stepSize, repeat twice
repeat 2 [forward :stepSize wait 1]
end
```

Code—Again

Now we can write the code, then test it again.

Let's build it step by step. One way to do it involves creating another local variable (a variable used just in this procedure) to store the number that is half of what's in **dizziness**. Remember how to create and name a variable? We use **local**, like this:

```
local "halfDizziness
```

Then we need to put into that variable half of **what's in dizziness**, or **:dizziness**. How do we get half of **what's in dizziness**?

```
quotient :dizziness 2
```

That looks like this using puzzle pieces:

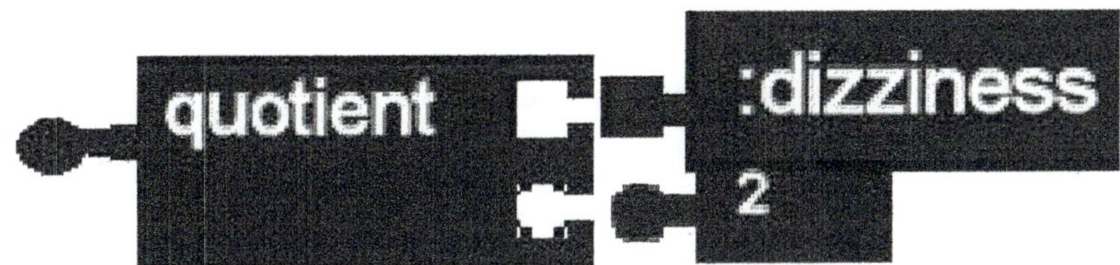

You see that **quotient** needs two inputs, one from **what's in dizziness**, and one is the number 2. It has one output, namely **what's in dizziness** divided by two.

Now, let's put that quotient into the variable **halfDizziness**, using **make**:

```
make "halfDizziness quotient :dizziness 2
```

Now, all we have to do is go back to our original code and substitute **what's in dizziness** and **what's in halfDizziness** for **100** and **50**. We had:

```
right difference random 100 50
```

Now we have:

```
right difference random :dizziness :halfDizziness
```

So our code looks like this now. I am underlining the changes.

```
to wander :stepSize :dizziness
  local "halfDizziness
  make "halfDizziness quotient :dizziness 2
  ;turn right by a random amount which could be negative
  ;turn right by a random amount up to dizziness
  right difference random :dizziness :halfDizziness
  ;move forward by stepSize, repeat twice
  repeat 2 [forward :stepSize wait 1]
end
```

Test

Now you can play with, I mean test your procedure. Here is my complete program:

```
===============================
to Main
  cc
  pd
  repeat 60 [wander 5 10]
end
===============================

to Start
  Main
end

to wander :stepSize :dizziness
  local "halfDizziness
  make "halfDizziness quotient :dizziness 2
  ;turn right by a random amount which could be negative
  ;turn right by a random amount up to dizziness
  right difference random :dizziness :halfDizziness
  ;move forward by stepSize, repeat twice
  repeat 2 [forward :stepSize wait 1]
end
```

Exercises

1. In the line in **Main** that calls **wander**, try these values for **wander**'s arguments: 5 & 10, 5 & 30, 5 & 300. What is happening to the turtle's dizziness, or change of heading?

2. Now, in the line in **Main** that calls **wander**, try these values for **wander**'s arguments: 5 & 10, 10 & 10, 50 & 10, 100 & 10. What is happening to the turtle's step size?

3. What do you need to do to make the turtle buzz crazily, moving fast and turning widely? Say it and do it.

4. Can you find any values for **dizziness** that cause an error? If you do, what do you think we should do about it?

5. Figure out a way to re-code so that we aren't using the local variable, **halfDizziness**, but get the job done anyway.

#7 Maze I

Decide on the Goal

Now we want to make an interactive game where a turtle, **t1**, is wandering through a maze, moving in the direction the user indicates. The user will use the arrow keys. When the user presses an arrow key, the turtle will move in that direction a few steps. To get the turtle to go a long way, the user will need to press the button a lot of times.

Open a new file. Using the drawing center, we will draw some maze lines. In the next lesson, we will add capability: when the turtle bumps into a maze line, the user loses and has to start over. The user wants to get the turtle through the maze to a destination: how about a second turtle dressed up as a castle (or a hut)? Eventually we will add roving spiders that want to "get" our turtle, and teleporter booths that send the turtle to some other spot in the maze.

Nicole's Maze

Draw up a Plan

This time, we are going to add a step: draw up a plan. We'll make a flow chart. A flow chart is a visual plan of what we are going to do. You read it from top to bottom; the program flows from one box to the next down the chart, with diamonds indicating decision points. Here is a start for our flow chart for the beginning part of the maze:

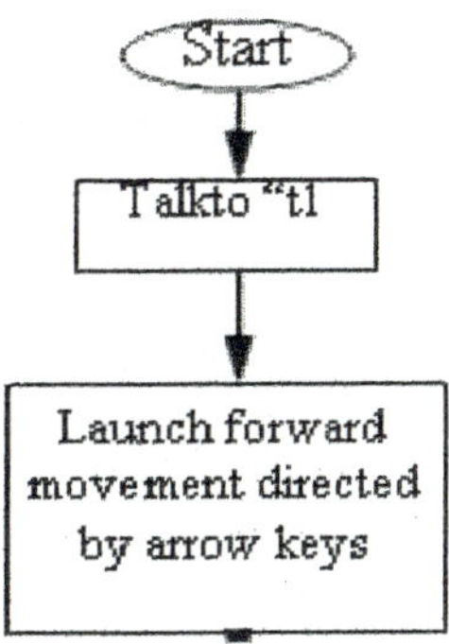

Sandbox for Necessary Knowledge

We want to move and turn the turtle by pushing the arrow keys. We'll need a lot of new information to figure out how to do this. First, how will we collect information from the keyboard?

Readchar is a built-in procedure that "reads" the input from the keyboard Let's check to see if it works. In the Command Center, type

    show readchar

and hit the **Enter** key. Now move your mouse arrow up to the graphics window and click there. Hit a letter key. Does the letter appear in the Command Center? It should. Put your cursor at the end of the **show readchar** line and press **Enter** again, to do it again. Now press one of the arrow keys. Oops! In the Command Center, we don't see an arrow; we get some symbol like &! This will vary depending on whether you are using a Mac or a PC. What's going on here?

Readchar is reading the character, but it is storing its information as a number! Then it is pulling the number out and using a code to figure out what it is, and it's getting mixed up about the arrow keys!

When you play at writing spy codes, you assign a number to each letter of the alphabet. It turns out there is a code like that built into computers. It's the ASCII code, which stands for the **American Standard Code for Information Interchange**, a code that assigns a number to each character. The problem is, it isn't an entirely standard code. The Mac and PC people use different code numbers for certain keys like arrow keys.

Logo has a built-in procedure called **ascii**. This procedure takes keyboard input from **readchar** and reports an ASCII code number for it.

Let's test this **ascii** procedure. In the Command Center, type

    show ascii "L

We're asking the computer to type the ASCII code for upper-case L in the Command Center. We get this response: **76**. This is the ASCII code for upper-case L.

Now, can you tell me the ASCII code for T? for the number 8? The letter H? h?

What we are most interested in is the codes for the arrow keys. But we can't type arrows into the Command Center. Can you figure out a way to get the computer to **show** the ASCII code in the Command Center for an arrow key? Hint: use **ascii** and **readchar**. Think about it and turn the page.

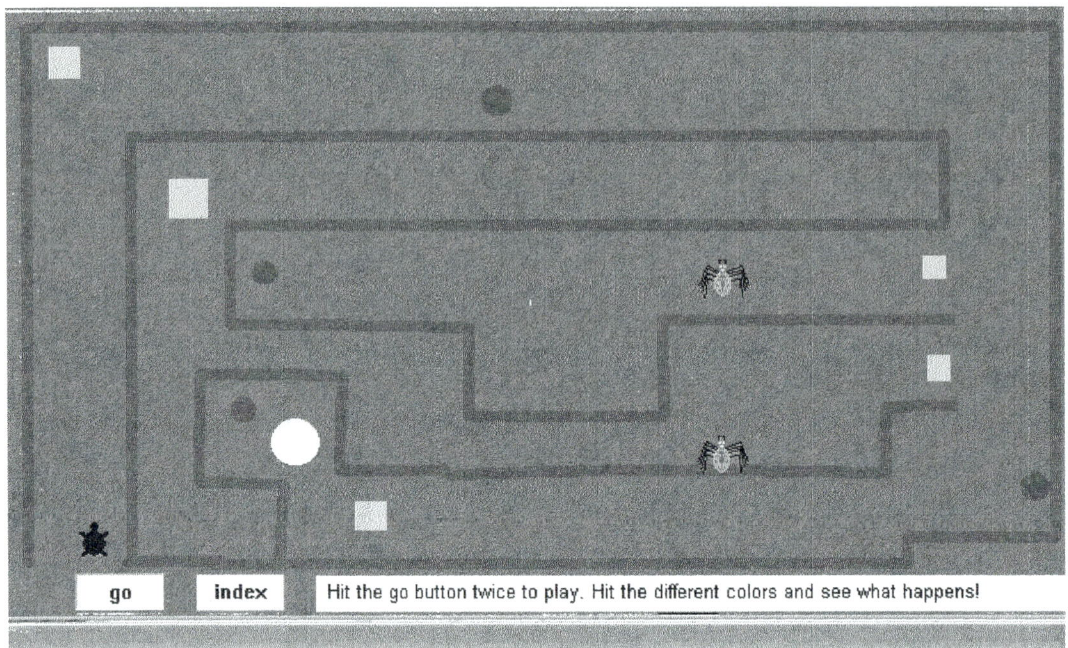

Hannah's Maze

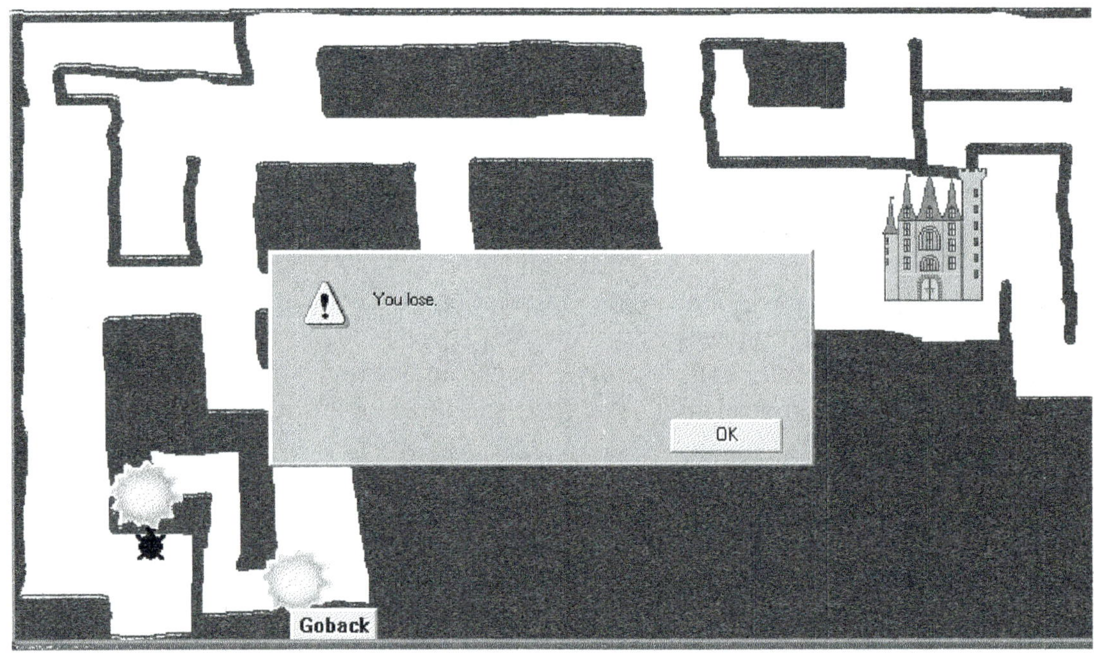

Robert's Maze

What we need is to use the procedure **ascii** to look at input from the keyboard from **readchar.**

Let's try this:

show ascii readchar

Then press **Enter**, move the cursor to the graphics window and click, and push any key. What number do you get? Do it again and press an arrow key. What number do you get?

We are interested in a very limited set of ASCII numbers: those that represent the arrows on our keyboard. Those numbers are different for Macintosh and PC. So we will set up a code system that works on either a Mac or PC keyboard. What it boils down to is this: 28 and 37 can be left, 29 and 39 can be right, 30 and 38 can be up, and 31 and 40 can be down.

Directing the Turtle's Head

First we will write a procedure to direct the turtle which way to point its head. We'll call the procedure **direct.**

In **Main**, **readchar** will pick up the keyboard input. Then **Main** will pass the keyboard information to **direct**. How will it do that? Do you remember how to pass information around in a program?

A variable will do the job nicely—a little pigeonhole to hold the information. **Main** will put the **readchar** information in the variable, and **direct** will pull it out, evaluate it, and use it. Let's call the variable **key**.

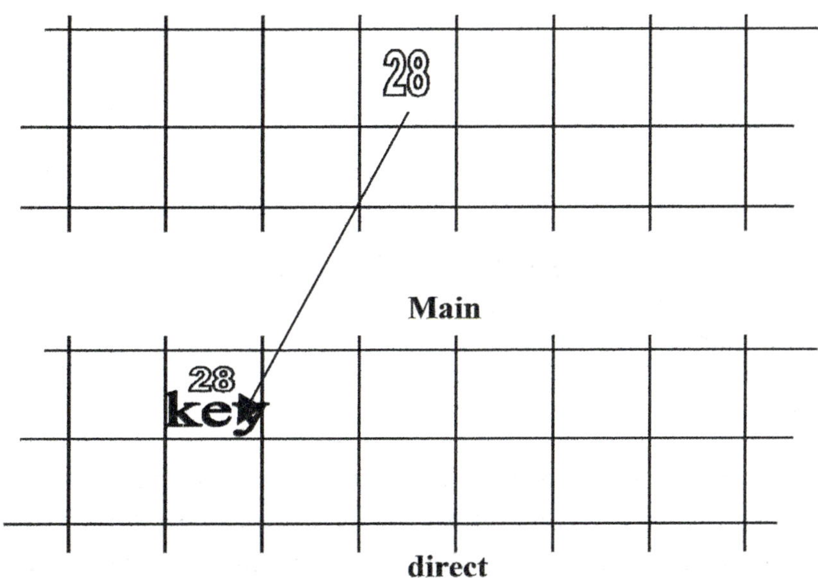

Main uses **readchar** to read "28" as the code for the key pressed. Then **Main** calls **direct** and sends it the value, storing it in the variable **key.**

Now our flow chart looks like this:

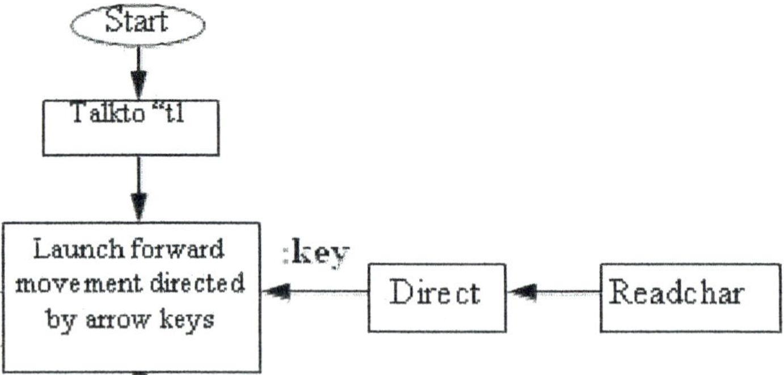

We will name the variable in the first line of the procedure **direct**, like this:

> **to direct :key**

When we call **direct** in **Main**, we would normally pass a number to it, like this:

> **to Main**
>
> **...**
>
> **direct 30**
>
> **...**
>
> **end**

But this time, we'll use **readchar** instead of the number 30. That way, whatever the keyboard input is will go into the variable, like this:

> **to Main**
>
> **...**
>
> **direct readchar**
>
> **...**
>
> **end**

In **Main**, we will read the keyboard input using **readchar** and then pass it to the procedure **direct**, storing it in the variable **key**. In **direct** we will evaluate it using **ascii** to see what the code number is. Then we will turn the turtle's head that way.

Here is our pseudocode for **direct**:

> **;If the code number is for the up arrow, set the turtle's heading to up (0).**
> **;If the code number is for the down arrow, set the turtle's heading to down (180).**
> **;If the code number is for the right arrow, set the turtle's heading to right (90).**
> **;If the code number is for the left arrow, set the turtle's heading to left (-90).**

It looks like we need four if-then statements, one for each arrow. But we actually need eight, because for each arrow key there are two possible code numbers (one for Mac, one for PC). Here is our finished code:

```
to direct :key
  if (ascii :key) = 28 [seth 270 fd 1]
  if (ascii :key) = 29 [seth 90 fd 1]
  if (ascii :key) = 30 [seth 0 fd 1]
  if (ascii :key) = 31 [seth 180 fd 1]
  if (ascii :key) = 37 [seth 270 fd 1]
  if (ascii :key) = 39 [seth 90 fd 1]
   if (ascii :key) = 38 [seth 0 fd 1]
  if (ascii :key) = 40 [seth 180 fd 1]
  if (:key = "s) [stopall] ;this means stop the program
end
```

Copy this procedure into your Procedures Page; it will be your starter. You'll also need to create:

- a **go** button in the graphics window

- on the Procedures Page a **go** procedure that calls **Main**

- a **Main** procedure. We will talk about that next.

Pseudocode

We will work in this way: we will create pseudocode that solves our problem. Then we will translate lines of pseudocode into Logo, then test. We will build the program by doing this over and over, adding in features as we go.

Here's some pseudocode to start with:

```
to Main
  ;talk to turtle 1
  ; launch a process that repeats many times a call to go forward a little bit
  ;use readchar to collect info from the keyboard, and also
  ;call direct, passing to it the information collected by readchar
end
```

First, we'll work on the first line of pseudocode. We'll need more information on **launch**. Do you remember the **launch** procedure from *Book 1?*

The Help vocabulary tells us this about **launch:**

launch

launch word-or-list-to-run

*Runs the input as an independent parallel process. If the process is launched from the Command Center, the cursor reappears immediately. Use cancel, the Cancel menu item, the Stop All menu item, or Ctrl+Break to stop the process. See also **forever**.*

Example:

launch [glide 1000 1]

Type the next instructions while the turtle is gliding.

rt 90

lt 90

Look at the very top of the entry: *Launch word-or-list-to-run.* What this means is that we need to use a word or a list as input for **launch.** (Remember, a **word** starts with a ", and a **list** is enclosed in [brackets like these]. **Launch** starts a process that we need to stop separately. I find it works best to **launch** something also using the **repeat** command, along with **forward.**

Now, we need a line of code that does all of these things:

> **;launches a process that repeats many times a call to go forward a little bit**
> **;uses readchar to collect info from the keyboard**
> **;calls direct, passing to it the information collected by readchar.**

Can you think of one? Work on it before you turn the page.

Crystal's Maze. The bee tries to get to the moon!

Here is mine:

launch [repeat 2000 [forward 3 direct readchar]]

Do you see how it works? Let's look at it from right to left. **Readchar** is taking one character of input from the keyboard. **Direct** is the procedure we made which needs one input (the keyboard character) and uses it to set the turtle's heading. Now, we have a little list of commands: go forward 3, and then change the turtle's heading using **direct** and the keyboard input. We will repeat this little set of commands 2,000 times, and we'll launch the whole process. This means that it will operate independently of other processes we might also launch.

Here's our next version of **Main**. I have underlined the new code.

```
to Main
  ;talk to turtle 1
  ;launch a process that repeats many times a call to go forward a little bit
  ;use readchar to collect info from the keyboard
  ;call direct, passing to it the information collected by readchar.
  launch [repeat 2000 [forward 3 direct readchar ] ]
end
```

Now, add a line of code to match the pseudocode for talking to turtle 1. Add the code for **to direct**, given earlier.

Now we have a program. Does it work?

On Page1, make a **go** button (using the icon that looks like a finger pushing a button). Using the drawing center under the paintbrush icon, draw some thick red lines or curves for your maze. You can make the maze more difficult by placing the lines close together. Go to Presentation Mode under the Gadgets menu at the top (or View menu in MicroWorlds EX). (To leave presentation mode, click on the black border.) Press the go button, and then start pushing the arrow keys to advance the turtle. Does it work? Work on yours before you look at mine on the next page. Be sure you use Presentation Mode for these mazes; otherwise they may not work properly. If your pen is still down, use the Command Center to tell the turtle pen up, or **pu.**

========

to Main
  ;talk to turtle 1
  talkto "t1
  ;launch a process that repeats many times a call to go forward a little bit
  ;use readchar to collect info from the keyboard
  ;call direct, passing to it the information collected by readchar.
  launch [repeat 2000 [forward 3 direct readchar]]
end

========

to direct :key
  if (ascii :key) = 28 [seth 270 fd 1]
  if (ascii :key) = 29 [seth 90 fd 1]
  if (ascii :key) = 30 [seth 0 fd 1]
  if (ascii :key) = 31 [seth 180 fd 1]
  if (ascii :key) = 37 [seth 270 fd 1]
  if (ascii :key) = 39 [seth 90 fd 1]
  if (ascii :key) = 38 [seth 0 fd 1]
  if (ascii :key) = 40 [seth 180 fd 1]
  if (:key = "s) [stopall]
end

to go
  Main
end

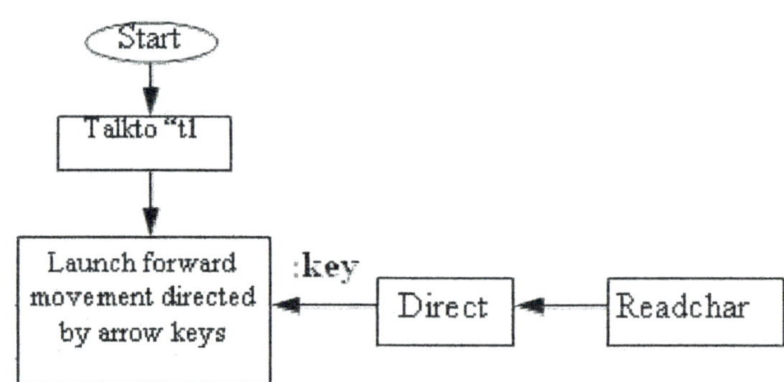

We have a maze starter now, but we have more to learn for this project.

#8 Maze II: Win or Lose?

Our starter maze does part of the assignment: it moves the turtle through some lines we have drawn, based on input to the keyboard's arrow keys. Now we want to do this part of the assignment: when the turtle bumps into a maze line, the user loses and has to start over.

Draw up a Plan

In our flow chart, we will need a diamond-shaped decision box as the next item down from the launch step. The decision box means the computer will decide whether a condition is true. If it is true, it goes down to the next steps (telling the user "you lose" and resetting the game). If it is false, it repeats the previous step. Like this:

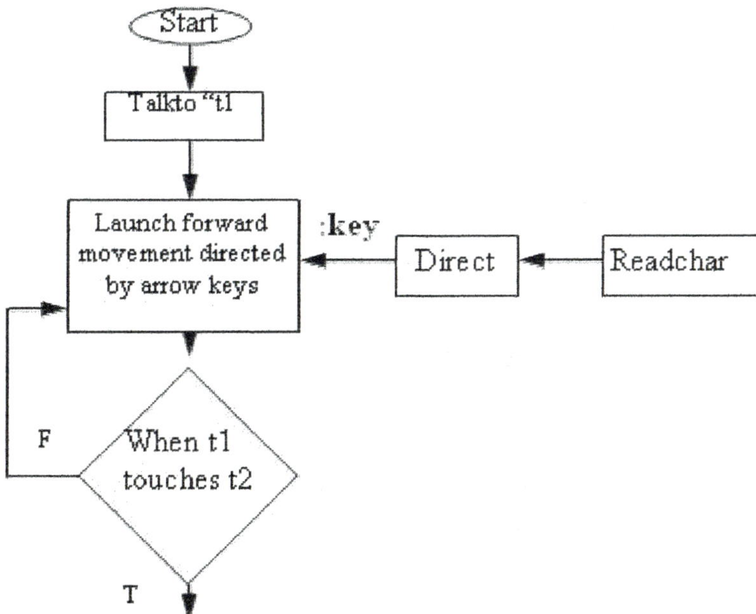

The condition will be this: did t1 run into a maze wall? Or more specifically, is its "colorunder" red?

First, More Sandboxing!

We need to learn more about some Logo procedures.

Colorunder is a procedure which has as output the number of the color the turtle is running into. So if the turtle runs into a **red** maze wall, the code can be detecting that by checking to see if **colorunder = 15.**

If **colorunder = 15** is true, we want to go on to the next step: announcing, "You lose."

Since we have launched a continuing process, though, we won't use

    if (colorunder=15)

That would only check once.

We have to use another procedure, **waituntil.**

The Help vocabulary tells us this about **waituntil:**

> *waituntil*
>
> *waituntil true-or-false-list-to-run*
>
> *Tells MicroWorlds to wait until true-or-false-list-to-run is true before running another instruction. The input must be an instruction list that reports either true or false when it is run. See **done?.***

The input for **waituntil** is a list, so it is in brackets. The input must be something that evaluates to true or false. All this means that our code needs to:

> **;launch a process that keeps going**
> **;waituntil [something is true]**
> **;announce "You lose!"**

First, let's eliminate our previous pseudocode. It seems to be getting in the way. Now we have:

```
to Main
 talkto "t1
 launch [repeat 2000 [forward 3 direct readchar ] ]
 end
```

Now, let's add some new pseudocode. We already have a line of code that launches the process. So now we need to put in the pseudocode for two more lines.

```
to Main
 talkto "t1
 launch [repeat 2000 [forward 3 direct readchar ] ]
 ;wait until the color under the turtle is color 15
 ;announce "You lose!"
 end
```

You need to translate the new lines into real code and put them under the pseudocode lines. Use **colorunder, waituntil,** and **announce.** Put yours together before you turn the page.

Your new code should look like this:

waituntil [colorunder = 15]
announce [You lose!]

More Pseudocode

Now we need more pseudocode, inserted after the **waituntil** line. We want to return the turtle to its starting point with head up.

Write in the pseudocode for this, and then turn the page to check it against mine.

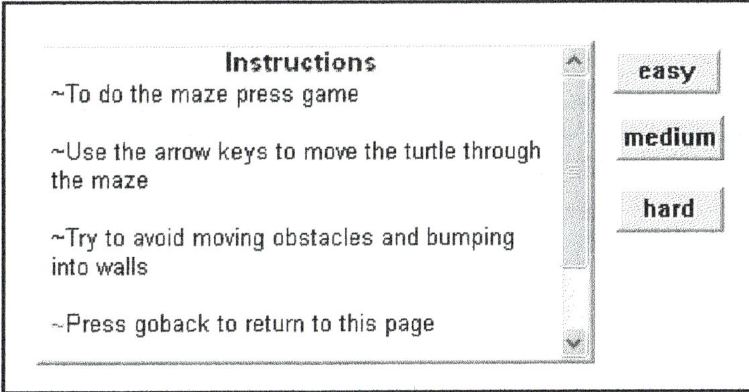

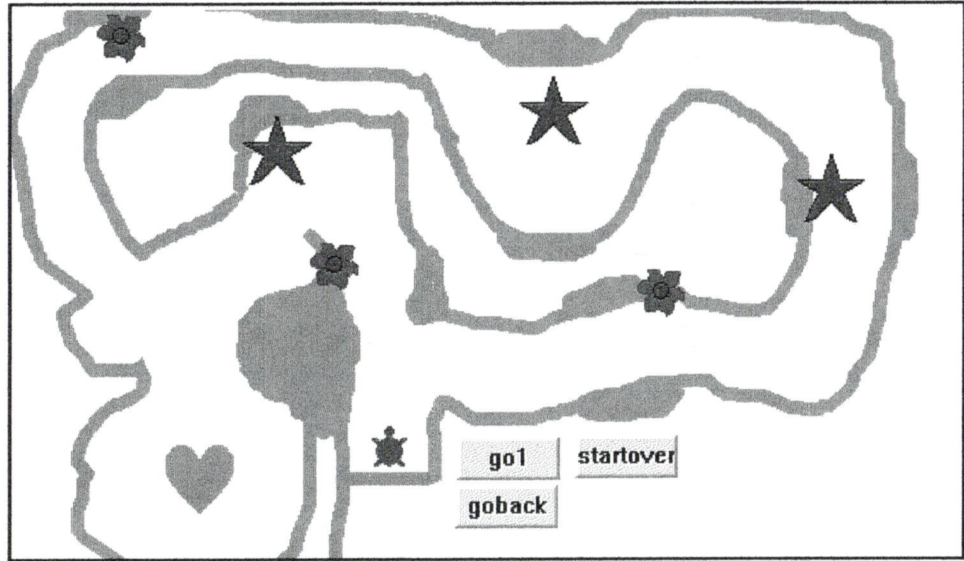

Elisa's Maze. Turtle tries to get to the heart of things.

```
to Main
  talkto "t1
  launch [repeat 2000 [forward 3 direct readchar ] ]
  waituntil [colorunder = 15]
  announce [You lose!]
  ;reset the game: move the turtle to a position above your go box and
  ;set the turtle's heading to 0
end
```

Our Plan

The plan now looks like this:

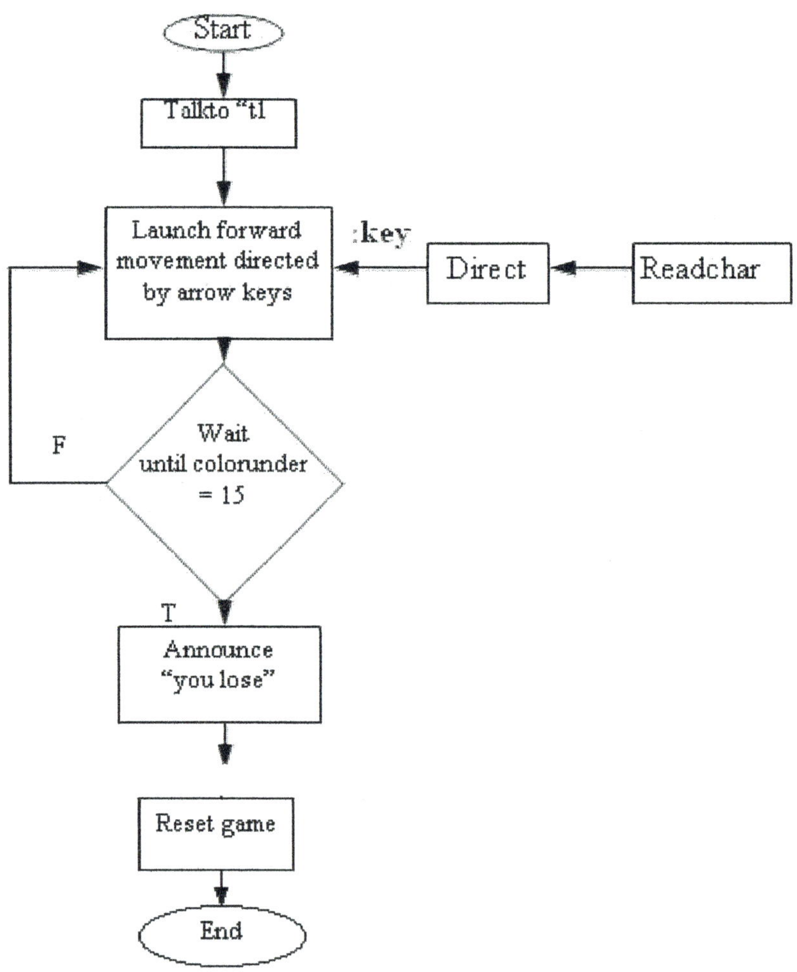

Some More Sandboxing

We need to make a **reset** procedure that returns **t1** to a place above your **go** button, and sets its heading to zero. Should it include "You lose"? I think not. That way we can use the **reset** procedure both when we lose and when we win.

Here is your pseudocode:

```
to reset
  ;return t1 to a place above your "go" button
  ;set its heading to zero
end
```

So we need to know a few more Logo procedures. How will we move the turtle to a position above the **go** button? **Setpos** will set the turtle's position. Look it up in the Help vocabulary to see how to use it. You need to know the coordinates of the position you want (numbers representing distance to the right and distance up from the center of the screen). But what are the coordinates of the spot above your **go** button? That will be different for each maze.

To find the coordinates of the position you want, move the turtle there using your mouse—pushing and holding down the mouse button to move the turtle around. Then go to the Command Center and type **show pos**. Note that in this case there is a space in the middle: **show** is the procedure, **pos** is the input. This will tell you the coordinates of that spot. Put those coordinates into your line using **setpos** (no space). Use the format on **setpos** from the help vocabulary.

Now, translate that to Logo, and call it from **Main**. You have a basic maze! Test your creation and tinker with it until it works. Remember to use Presentation Mode.

Exercises

Add these enhancements. First, add pseudocode to your code. Then translate it to Logo.

1. Make a second turtle in the shape of a castle as the destination in the maze. Use the turtle-hatching icon. This will be **t2**. You will want to shrink it down, using the magnifying glass with the minus sign. (The moving turtle is **t1**.) That way we can see the **t1** animation.

2. Look up these in the help vocabulary:

    when and
    touching?

    Create a line in **Main** that changes the shape of **t1** when it touches **t2**. We want this to happen *before* the ending sequence—where the computer is waiting for the turtle to run into a red line to reset the game. Where should the new line go? Sketch the flow chart we have so far and add this diamond-shaped decision box to it in the right place.

3. Make a procedure called **win** that provides a reward for the winner—the one who reaches the maze destination. First it will announce "You win!" Next, how about some animation

for the winner? Make this procedure change the shape of **t1** into a cloud, wait a little, and then change **t1** into another shape. To find the name of a shape, go to the Shape Center (dog's head icon in MicroWorlds 2.0). Pause the mouse over a shape to see its name and number. You can use either the name (for example, **bee1**) or the number (**11**) to call it.

In the **win** procedure, remember to talk to **t1**, then use **setsh**, wait a bit, and use **setsh** again.

Test it by typing **win** in the Command Center, and pressing **Enter**. Once you get that working, call it from **Main**. You will need to change the line in **Main** that uses **when** and **touching?**

4. Now, make some adjustments to **win**. Change it so that you choose a shape randomly the second time you call **setsh**. Use **random** as input. Look up **random** before you use it. You take advantage of the fact that the shapes all have numbers to call shapes randomly. You have to choose a number as input for **random** that makes sense based on what the shape numbers are; an input of 50,000 won't get you anywhere!

   Enhance **win** and **reset** so that after the turtle changes shapes, the turtle is returned to its turtle shape and goes back to its starting place. Now, play with your game! Save it as Mymaze. We will pick up here with the next lesson.

5. Draw additions to our flow chart to describe what we have made so far. You will want to make two pathways coming down from the one box that says "launch forward movement directed by arrow keys," to show that two things are happening at the same time: the **waituntil** and the **when**, and both can lead to the end of the game. Once you try a sketch, take a look at mine in the answer key.

Prince/Princess Project:

Save this project separately from the maze we have been working on. Let's imagine our turtle is a prince or princess changed into a turtle by a witch. The turtle really wants to get to the castle at the center of the maze in order to be changed back into a prince or princess. Ask the user whether the user would prefer a prince or princess. Store this information in a variable and then use it to change the turtle into a boy or a girl, as appropriate to the choice, when the turtle reaches the castle.

Hints for **Main**: First, create a variable called **preference** to use within **Main**, using **local**. If you can't remember how to use **local**, look it up in the Help vocabulary. You will also need to use **announce**, **question**, and **ifelse**. Look those up too, to jog your memory. If the user answers B for boy, you will need to make the value in the variable preference match the shape number for boy. Otherwise, you need to make the value match the shape number for girl.

Hints for **win:** Change **win** so that it takes a variable passed to it. **Setsh** will use the value in this variable to set the shape for **t1**. So, when you call **win**, the shape will become a boy or a girl depending on what value is stored in the variable.

#9 Maze III

Assignment

- Add to your Mymaze maze (not the prince/princess maze) at least two moving obstacles. These will be turtles wearing shapes. They could be a fireball (sun) or a spider that you create. We will call them spiders. In your code, make a spider turn 180 degrees every time it hits a maze wall.

- When the **t1** turtle bumps into a spider, the game announces "You lose." Then it resets: the turtle goes back to the start spot with its head up, the same result as when **t1** hits a maze line.

- Put instructions for the user in a text box, something like "Use arrow keys to direct turtle."

Let's work on the first requirement: add two moving obstacles. Make the obstacles turn 180 degrees every time they hit a maze wall.

First you need to create your moving obstacles. To draw a spider shape, double click on one of the empty spots in the Shape Center and then use the drawing tools to make and name your spider shape. Or use a sun or some other shape. "Hatch" two more turtles (**t3** and **t4**). Go to the Shape Center, click on the shape, and then click on the turtle. This puts the new "clothes" on the turtle so it looks like that shape. Move the turtles around by dragging them with the pointer. Put them at likely spots in your maze.

We will have separate sections of code addressed to each turtle: **t1, t3,** and **t4** (**t2** is your destination castle and won't be moving). Here is some pseudocode for example:

> **;talk to t1**
> **;launch a movement for t1**
> **;end that movement under a certain condition.**

For ending the movement, we first used **waituntil**. But when we are talking to multiple turtles all launched into various movements, **waituntil** doesn't work well. There is a similar built-in procedure that we can use. That is **when**.

To jog your memory, look **when** up in the Help vocabulary:

***when** true-or-false-instruction-list instruction-list*

*Starts a parallel process that repeatedly tests whether the first instruction list reports true or false. If it reports true, the second instruction list is run. To stop a **when**, use cancel on the true-or-false-instruction-list, the Cancel menu item, the Stop All menu item, or press Ctrl+Break.*

Example:

when [ycor > 50][bk 20]

In other words, it launches a process that keeps checking the condition in the first set of brackets to see if it is true. When it is true, it runs the instruction inside the second set of brackets.

What's the difference between **when** and **waituntil**? Both **when** and **waituntil** keep checking the condition to see if it is true. When it is true, the **waituntil** procedure simply lets the computer go past it to the next lines of code. It's like **waituntil** is a traffic cop, holding up traffic till the light turns green. When it turns green, the traffic moves on.

When, on the other hand, checks for the green light and then lets the traffic do exactly one thing or list of things. This might be a little neater for us, with our multiple turtles.

We need to use **when** and some procedures we make to cause the user to either win or lose, depending on whether they meet the winning condition (**t1** touches **t2**), or the losing condition (**t1** touches a red line).

For losing, we will make a **lose** procedure, which uses the **reset** procedure we already made. When the condition is true (**t1** is touching a red line), the computer will run **lose. Lose** will announce "You lose!" and then will call **reset.**

For winning, we will use the procedure we already made, **win**. In **win, t1** turns into a cloud and then into something else, waits a bit, goes back to the start with head up, and announces "You win!" Then it calls **reset.**

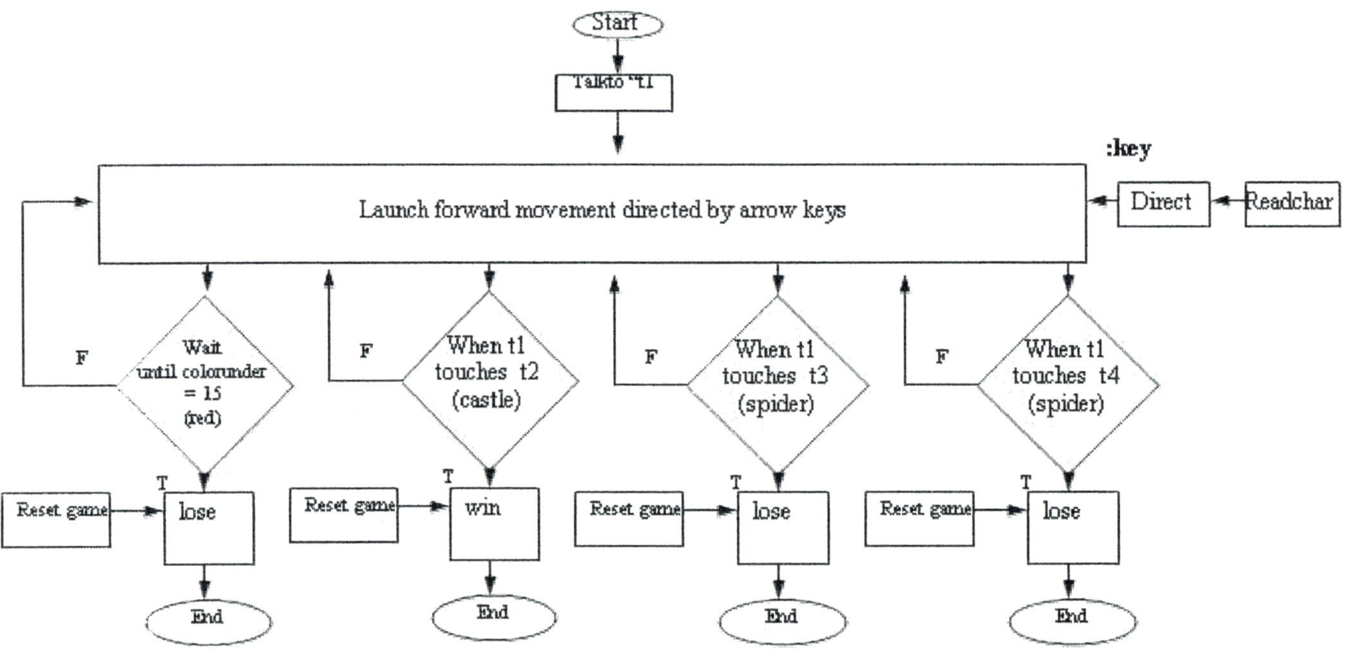

What do you think of the diagram above? Notice that it has four decision-checkers working at once, each represented by a diamond. All are talking to **t1**, because they follow the command to **talkto "t1** at the beginning. Each one leads to an end to the game. Does it represent our program?

I see two problems with it:

1. Where do we launch **t3** and **t4**? They need to be moving back and forth, turning 180 degrees when **colorunder = 15**. Let's put them at the beginning. Our launched movements run at the same time, so we will put them alongside each other.

2. We could use **when** instead of **waituntil**, now that we have changed what happens after **waituntil**. Instead of several commands, now it is just one procedure. Using the same commands (**when**) everywhere would be a little neater, wouldn't it?

Take a look at this diagram now. Will it do?

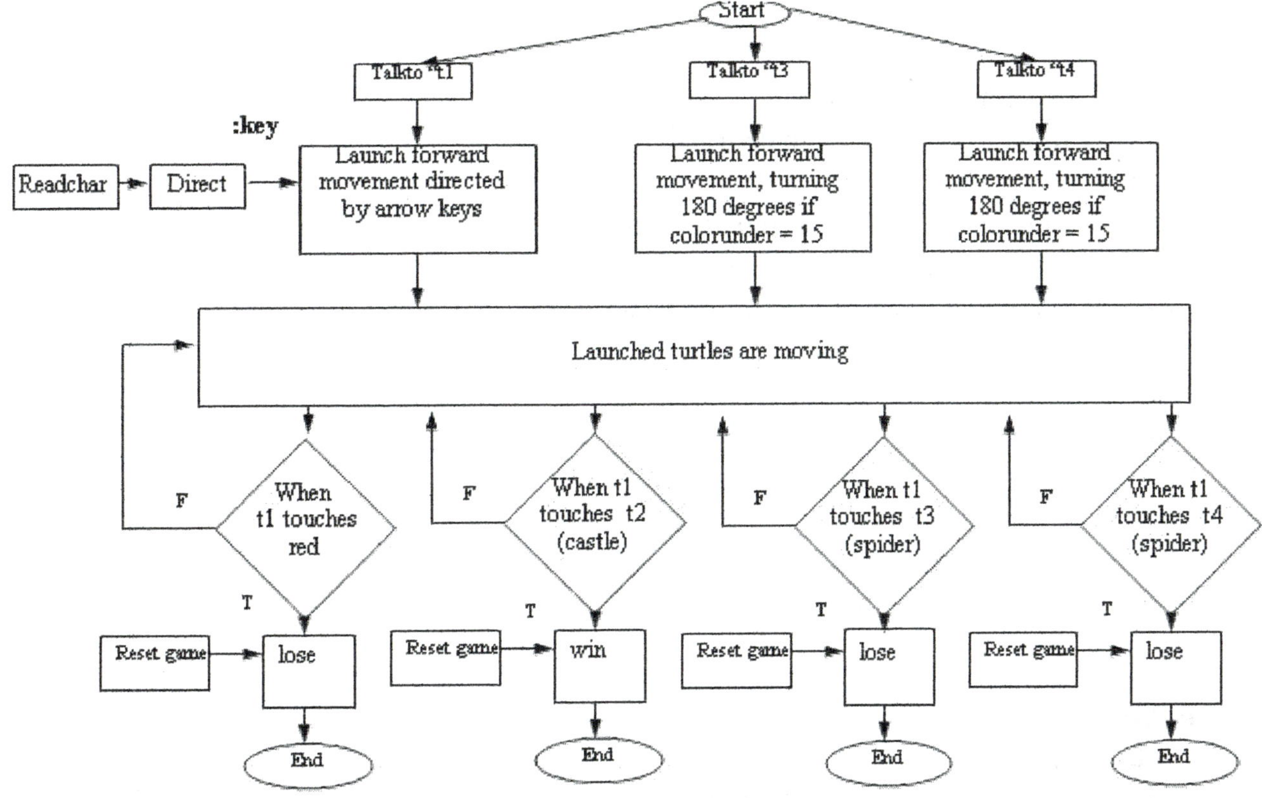

I want you to write some pseudocode in **Main** to match this diagram. DO NOT TURN THE PAGE until you have a draft. It doesn't have to be perfect! Just work on it for a little while, to get the problem into your head.

Here is my pseudocode:

```
to Main
;talk to t1
;launch forward movement, and turn using arrow keys

;talkto t3
;launch forward movement
;when t3 touches red, turn 180 degrees

;talkto t4
;launch forward movement
;when t4 touches red, turn 180 degrees

;when t1 touches red, lose (a separate procedure)
;when t1 touches t2, win (a separate procedure)
;when t1 touches t3, lose (a separate procedure)
;when t1 touches t4, lose (a separate procedure)

end
```

Code

Let's recall our Mymaze code from the last lesson:

```
==========
to Main
  talkto "t1
  launch [repeat 2000 [forward 3 direct readchar ] ]
  when [touching? "t1 "t2] [win]
  waituntil [colorunder = 15]
  announce [You lose!]
  reset
end
==========
to direct :key
  if (ascii :key) = 28 [seth 270 fd 1]
  if (ascii :key) = 29 [seth 90 fd 1]
  if (ascii :key) = 30 [seth 0 fd 1]
  if (ascii :key) = 31 [seth 180 fd 1]
  if (ascii :key) = 37 [seth 270 fd 1]
  if (ascii :key) = 39 [seth 90 fd 1]
  if (ascii :key) = 38 [seth 0 fd 1]
```

```
  if (ascii :key) = 40 [seth 180 fd 1]
  if (:key = "s) [stopall]
end

to go
  Main
end

to win
  announce [You win!]
  talkto "t1
  setsh "cloud wait 2
  setsh random 60 wait 10
  reset
end

to reset
  talkto "t1
  setpos [-319 -164]
  seth 0
  setsh "turtle
end
```

First of all, let's add a procedure, **to lose**. It will announce "You lose!" and call **reset**. Go ahead and code that one.

Now, let's look at **Main**. We're going to start with our new pseudocode and re-write **Main**. First we'll take the new pseudocode and plug in useful lines of code from the previous Mymaze.

```
to Main
;talk to t1
  talkto "t1
;launch forward movement, and turn using arrow keys
  launch [repeat 2000 [forward 3 direct readchar ] ]
```

Can you come up with code for the next two lines of pseudocode? Our forward movement will use **launch, repeat**, and **forward.** Use a large number for the **repeat.**

```
;talkto t3
;launch forward movement
```

Now, code the next line, using **when, colorunder,** and **right**:

```
;when t3 touches red, turn 180 degrees
```

Now, code the next three lines, using the previous three as a model:

> **;talkto t4**
> **;launch forward movement**
> **;when t4 touches red, turn 180 degrees**

Now, code the next line. You will need to **talkto "t1** again. Then you will need **when** and **colorunder**.

> **;when t1 touches red, lose (a separate procedure)**

The next line is already done for us, from the previous Mymaze:

> **;when t1 touches t2, win (a separate procedure)**
> *when [touching? "t1 "t2] [win]*

Now, code the last two lines, using the one above as a model.

> **;when t1 touches t3, lose (a separate procedure)**
> **;when t1 touches t4, lose (a separate procedure)**

> **end**

You'll want to delete the pseudocode lines once you get the thing working.

Remember this part of the assignment?

- Put instructions for the user in a text box, something like "Use arrow keys to direct turtle."

Make a text box (using the icon that shows a box filled with the letters "abc"). Put in some instructions for the user. Move the box to a good spot by holding down the left mouse button and dragging the box around.

Now, pull it all together and run the maze with the spiders! Save it again as Mymaze.

Extra Credit

Use a slider (a picture of a button that slides) to let the user adjust the speed of the sun/spider. Hatch a slider from the toolbox at the left, sixth icon down—it looks like a belt with buckle. The new slider will be called **slider1**. Use this name instead of a number input, for instance **forward slider1.** It will need to be in the code that launches the movements for the spiders, **t3** and **t4.** Now, adjust the slider and play around with it. Save this as slidermaze, and don't use it for the next lesson!

#10 Maze IV

Assignment

We will enhance Mymaze some more. It now will have three difficulty levels, involving the spiders' speed. We will need one duplicate page for each difficulty level, and also an index page to start from. This will have buttons on it that take us to the easy, medium and difficult pages. We'll also need buttons on those pages to go back to the index page. We will call the index page **Page1** because, in MicroWorlds, any project starts with the one called **Page1** when it loads. We want it to start with the index, so we will call that **Page1**.

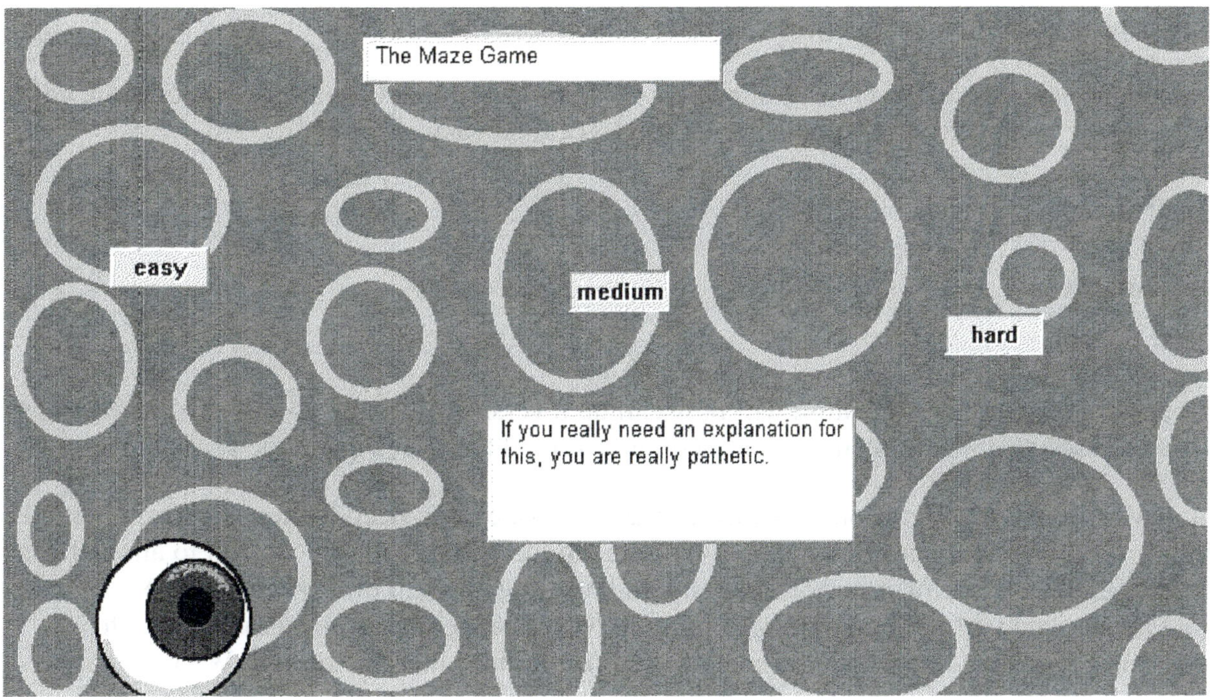

Page1 from Hannah's Maze

Get to Work

We'll be working with multiple pages in our project for this. Notice that there is a **Pages** menu at the top of the screen. When you click on it, you see you have options to create new pages and to name pages. We will need to do both.

Save your maze under another name for backup, just in case you mess up. Now, in the Mymaze file, create three duplicate pages. To do this, go to the **Pages** menu, and click on **duplicate page**. This makes a new page just like the old one, only this one is called **Page2**. Click **duplicate** two more times. Now you have **Page1, Page2, Page3**, and **Page4**, all the same.

But these names aren't descriptive. Using the Pages menu, go to **Page2**. Then under the Pages menu select **name,** and name the page **easypage**. Go to **Page3** and name it **mediumpage**, and go to **Page4** and name it **hardpage**.

Now you have pages named **Page1, easypage, mediumpage, and hardpage.** These are more than names. They are commands! If you go to the Command Center and type one of the names, that page appears. So we could put the name into our code as a command. We want to call these pages using buttons on the index page, **Page1**.

There are two ways to do this. We could name the button the same as the page. When we push the button, the page comes up. Or we could do it indirectly. Each button could call a procedure we write. The procedure can then call the page name, and can also call a version of **Main** just for that page. Let's do it that way.

Using the Page menu, go to **Page1** and clear the graphics by typing **cg** in the Command Center. Use the scissors icon to get rid of the turtles and the **go** button. Now, using the button creator tool on the left, create three buttons, one named **easy**, one named **medium**, and one named **hard**. Drag them around the page to create a nice arrangement. Decorate the page too.

Now we need to make procedures to call our pages. On the Procedures Page, make a procedure called **to easy**. It tells the computer what to do when the button called **easy** is pushed.

```
to easy
 easypage
 Maineasy
end
```

You notice that pushing the **easy** button will now call up a version of **Main**, so we won't need any **go** buttons (which used to do that). You can cut them out from all the pages using the scissors icon.

So, what is **Maineasy**? It's a version of **Main** for the **easy** page. You need to create it. Highlight all of your **Main** procedure and hit **control-c** to copy it to the hidden clipboard. Now scroll to another part of your Procedures Page (remember, procedures should be in alphabetical order, except for **Main** first, so this should be near the top!). Hit **control-v** to paste it. Now change the name on the old one to **Maineasy**. Paste another copy. Make the new ones **Mainmedium** and **Mainhard**. We will make changes to make them different from each other in a little while.

We need something else: a way to return from each game page to **Page1**. On each of the game pages, make a button called **index.** To go with it, you'll need to make a procedure for **to index** using this pseudocode:

```
to index
 ;go to Page1
end
```

Put real code in to replace the pseudocode.

Test it. Make adjustments if you need to.

At the moment, you have three different maze pages for your game, with different names but otherwise the same. We need to change the speed of the spiders on each page, in **Maineasy, Mainmedium,** and **Mainhard.** Remember the spiders are **t3** and **t4**. In **Maineasy, t3** and **t4** should have the same slow speed. In **Mainmedium**, **t3** and **t4** should both be moving faster. In **Mainhard,** they should be moving even faster. You can shorten the waits to speed things up. Remember, **t1** is moving three turtle steps with every push of the arrow key. So on your easy page, the spiders could be moving three steps and waiting three. On the medium page, they could move three steps and wait two. On the hard page, they could move four steps and wait two, for example. You can make changes in the way the mazes are drawn on the three pages, too.

Now, test your spider speeds. The easy page should be easy, the medium page medium difficulty, and the hard page hard but not impossible. You don't want to have no users because your game is too hard! So adjust the speeds until the reality matches the name for each page. You can make the spiders smaller, too, using the magnifying glass with the minus sign in it.

Put It on the Internet!

Get ready to put your maze on the Internet. You can ask us at Motherboard Books to put it on our Web site (email your two files to info@motherboardbooks.com), or you can put it on your own. First, to play a MicroWorlds game using your Internet browser, you need to download a Webplayer plug-in. Go to www.microworlds.com/Webplayer/index.html and download the Webplayer for your version of MicroWorlds.

Now you need to make an HTML file as a companion to your maze file. At www.microworlds.com, select the project library button on the left side. When in the project library, choose the "post your projects" button on the upper right. Follow the directions to some HTML code. Copy the code, and open Wordpad or Notepad and paste it there. Save it with the same name as your maze, except with an .html extension, for example, joymaze.html. Follow the directions on the Web site for changing the code to match your project. Save it in the same folder as your maze. The maze and the matching HTML file constitute your Web page. You can play it by finding the HTML file through your My Computer icon and double clicking on it.

Exercises

1. Add teleporter booths. Here's how: put a box of another color into the maze. When the **t1** turtle hits the color, it jumps to a different spot in the maze. To find the coordinates of the spot you want to teleport to, move the turtle there using the mouse, and then type **show pos** in the Command Center.

2. Create animations using a list of shapes with **setsh** and repeated calls to **forward**.

    a. Have the **t1** turtle animate when it reaches the goal.

    b. Make an animation for the spiders (**t3** and **t4**) as they move, giving realistic motion.

    c. Animate the **t1** turtle as it goes through the maze. One possibility: make it look like Pac-Man, an ancient videogame hero who looks like a yellow cookie. You can make new shapes by double clicking on the blank shapes in the Shapes Center and using drawing tools to construct them.

#11 Get Ready, Get Set for Race

Race is a two-person geography game. Two vehicles are racing in a geographic setting of some kind—the Sahara desert, the moon, Los Angeles, or whatever. To move his vehicle, the player has to answer a question correctly.

We will pull in an image of the setting for the background. Vehicle 1 will go ¼ of the way across the screen every time player 1 correctly answers a question concerning the scene in the background, and the same for vehicle 2 and player 2. The questions alternate between player 1 and player 2. The vehicles can be cars for Los Angeles, or rockets for the Moon, or whatever seems appropriate for other scenes. When someone gets to the finish line, a third turtle which has been hidden shows itself and does a little animation. Of course the object is to get there first!

Construction involves several steps. Today we will do the preparation part.

First, you need a background picture. Select a background from the MicroWorlds disk. Or you can pull an image from the Internet. Here's how you do that. We need to find a picture that is free, that is, which the copyright owner has designated as no charge for us to use. You can check out www.picturesfree.org. Or go to www.google.com and click on the word "images" just above the blank search line. Now, in the images search, type in "free" and a keyword for what you want to find. If we are looking for the Arizona desert, we could type in "free desert arizona" and see what we get. Once you find a free picture you like, and where the owner has clearly said you can use it free on the Internet (not just your desktop), go to your file menu and use **Save As** to download it to your computer. Save it as a .gif or .bmp. Then open your MicroWorlds file and go to the **File** menu, then **import**. Find the picture file's location and import the picture to your project. If the picture is the wrong size, you will have to re-size it using photo editing software such as Microsoft Picture It. If this sounds like too much trouble, just pick something off the MicroWorlds disk! Or, here's a third option: use the drawing tools to draw a background. One student in our class "drew" Antarctica, which is mostly white, with a few ice floes and so on. His racers were penguins. Use your imagination!

Next, create two new turtles using the drawing center and some turtle shape blanks. Give them simple names. They can look like race cars, jackrabbits, eagles, or whatever matches your background. Make them similar but in contrasting colors.

Now, write eight easy questions in a word processor. They should have one- or two-word answers that concern the place you picture. Check your spelling and save. You will copy and paste them into your code shortly.

Finally, consider how you are going to tackle this problem. Make a draft of a flow chart showing the steps you think we'll need. Use a block for a question, and a decision diamond for deciding what to do with the answer. Indicate that this question-answer repeats four times for each user. Show this to your teacher.

#12 Race II

Here are our game specifications:

- The game starts with a **Start** button. It has a thick finish line drawn using the drawing center.

- The game has two users and two turtles. The turtles move a distance to the right (or up) each time the corresponding user answers a question correctly.

- There are four easy questions for each user. After four correct answers, a turtle reaches the finish line.

- If a racing turtle crosses the finish line, a third turtle which has been hidden becomes visible and does an animation of your choice. (This is a procedure called **win**.)

- The racing turtles return to the starting gate when a user presses **Start**. Also, the animated turtle returns to its starting position. (This is a procedure called **setup**.)

One thing to keep in mind as you design your game is that the questions will appear in a large rectangle in the middle of the screen, which will tend to hide the racers if they are also crossing that part of the screen. You can solve this problem by moving the racers to the top or bottom of the screen, or by providing long waits between questions so the user can see where the racer is.

Our flow chart will begin with **Start**, **setup**, and a question block, and then a decision diamond for the answer. If the answer is true, the turtle moves forward. If it is false, we announce "Oops!" and tell the user what the right answer was. In either case, we then go on to the next question. Work again on your sketch of this, and then turn the page to see mine.

Paul's Race: The Winner! A ghost appears and walks to the top of the mountain.

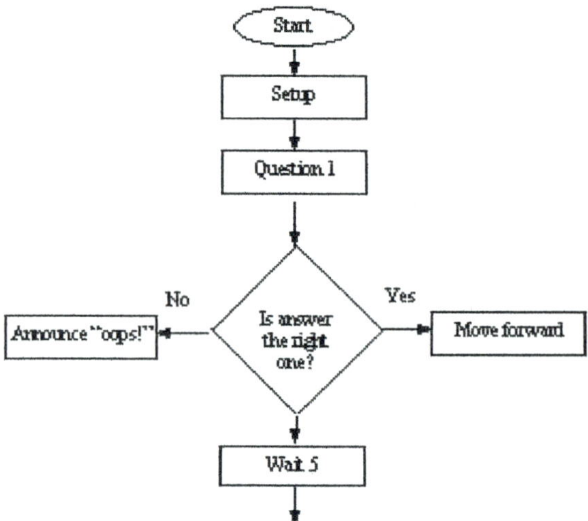

This is a good start for the first question! Now let's add Question 2, just like it.

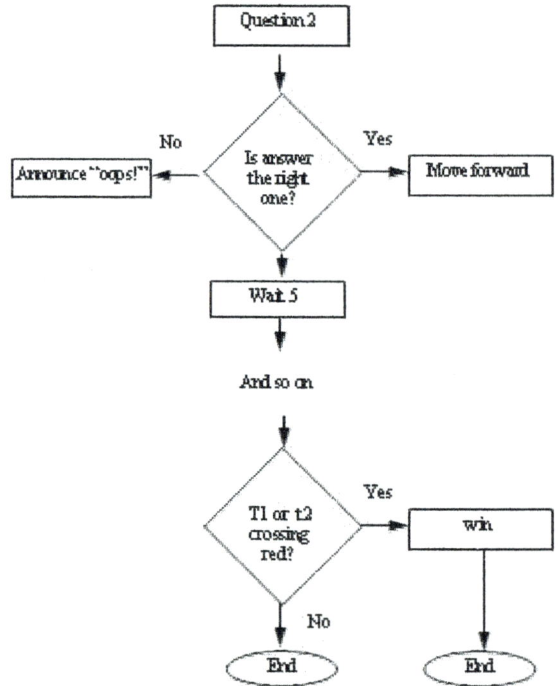

Did your flow chart look a lot like this? I hope so.

Now, we need to translate the flow chart to Logo code for **Main**. For the question, we will use the command **question**. Look it up in the Help vocabulary if you need to.

Next we need to evaluate **answer**, where the user's answer is stored. The flow chart shows a decision diamond with the question, "Is answer the right one?" There are two possible outcomes: right answer and wrong answer. Can you code this? Look up **if** and **ifelse**, to jog your memory. Don't turn the page until you have sketched out some code.

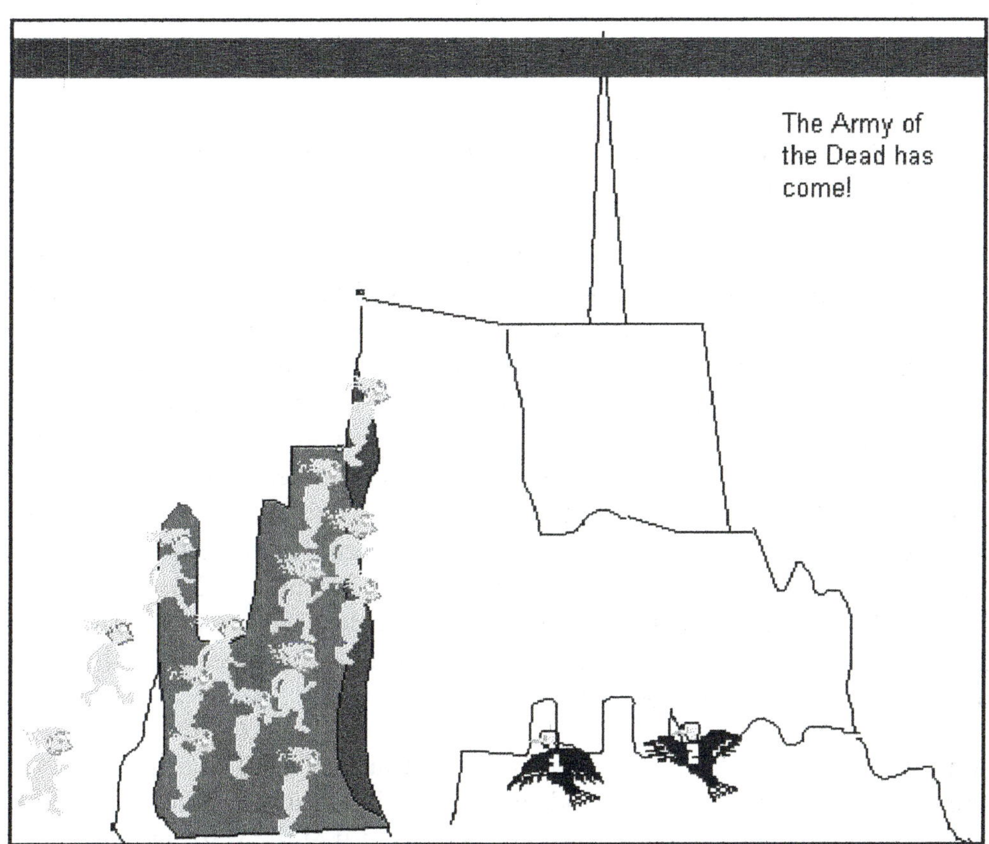

Paul's Race, Page Two (after winning). The army of the dead shows up!

If the user gives the right answer, we can write:

if (answer = "|Mount Vernon|) [talkto "t1 forward 170]

Notice the vertical lines around and quote mark before the two-word answer. If the answer is only one word, you can just use a quote mark before the word, like this:

if (answer = "Vernon) [talkto "t1 forward 170]

Let's work in the other case, where the answer is not equal to Mount Vernon. Can you figure out what to write?

ifelse (answer = "|Mount Vernon|) [talkto "t1 forward 130] [announce [Oops! The right answer was Mount Vernon.]]

For the questions, copy and paste from the list of questions you made already. Address the right user in your question, too, like this:

question [Player 1, What is the name of George Washington's home?]

We also need to make sure the racers can cross the screen all the way to the finish line, if they get the answers all right. Here are two ways to do it:

1. Using **show pos,** check the coordinates of the start point and the end point. To do this, put **t1** at the start point, go to the Command Center, type **talkto "t1 show pos**, and write down the coordinates. Now move **t1** to the finish line and type **show pos** in the Command Center. Write down those coordinates. The first number is the x coordinate, and the second is the Ycoordinate. You need to subtract the x coordinates for a horizontal race. (X measures horizontal distance across the screen, and Ymeasures vertical distance.) For instance, your start coordinates might be [-332 -129] and your end coordinates might be [342 -135]. Looking at the first numbers only, your turtle will have to go to the right 332 steps to get to the invisible zero reference line in the middle of the screen. It will have to go another 342 steps to get to the finish line. So the distance traveled is 332 plus 342, or 678 steps. We are asking each turtle four questions to get there, so we divide 678 by 4 to get 169 and a remainder, so we'll round it up to 170. In short, each time we answer a question correctly, we need to go 170 steps. It may be different for yours.

2. If you don't understand what I just did, you can use trial and error to arrive at a step length. Adjust the step length until the turtle lands on the finish line after going forward four times. You can do this in the Command Center—talk to **t1**, put it at the starting place, and tell it to go forward 170, forward 170, and so on four times. Did it land on the line? If not, change the number. Or redraw the line! You can also make the line into a colored rectangle. What's important is that the winner be sitting on the color red (or other color you choose).

You should have code in place for questions. Test it. Does it work? If not, make adjustments. You can "comment out" the setup line by putting a semicolon in front of it, because it doesn't work yet. Don't forget to remove the semicolon once you actually write the code for **setup.**

Now we need to write the code in **Main** that calls **win**, the animation for the winner. In our flow chart there is a decision diamond here. Can you translate that to code? We need to include something else: an instruction to talk to both **t1** and **t2** before we check the color under the turtle. Look in the MicroWorlds Help under **talkto** to see how to address two turtles at once.

Now that you have **Main** written, write **win**. Here are requirements:

- Talk to **t3.**

- Show turtle (**st**) and animate it. Remember to use **setsh** and a list of shapes, then make repeated calls to **forward.**

Now write **setup**. Here are the requirements:

- Talk to **t1**; set its position at the starting gate using **setpos** and the coordinates you got from **show pos** in the Command Center. Set its heading. (Look these up in the Help vocabulary: **setpos** and **seth**.

- Do the same for **t2**.

- Put **t3** at its starting point; this could be on the finish line. Set its heading. Hide **t3** (**ht** is for hide turtle).

Test your code. Does it work? Make adjustments until it does.

Exercise

What if the player doesn't guess four questions right? We need to figure out what to do then. How about announcing "No winners!" Can you figure out where to put that command? Think about it and test your idea.

Crystal's Race: Clifford and T-Bone go for a tiny bone that flips around on winning.

#13 Race III

We're going to add some fun stuff to our game. Let's make a wild set of animations for winning. Here's our next requirement:

- When someone wins, nine turtles appear and run through animations, for example, from a yellow ball to a small ball of fire to a larger ball of fire to a largest ball of fire, and over again.

- Text appears announcing "You won!"

- When the animations are over and the user clicks **Start**, the game resets to original condition.

There's an easy way to take care of the multiple animations and the reset: we'll put the multiple animations on a different page. When someone wins, we go to that page. When someone clicks **Start** again, we go back to **Page1**.

Here's how: Go to **Page1**. Under the **Pages** menu, select **duplicate page.** Now you have another page, **Page2**, that looks just like **Page1**. You can draw on it to make it look somewhat different. You can add some text, such as "You won!!!" Hatch turtles all over the place. Keep track of how many you have. Now, go to the shapes center and make some shapes that go with your theme. You can copy digital pictures and paste them into the turtle shape blocks. Or you can make an explosion. Use the spray can and spray some red and yellow dots. For another shape, make the "explosion" bigger, and for a third, even bigger. You can also make a yellow disk. An animation could cycle through these shapes: disk to small explosion to larger to largest. Or the explosion could start small and get bigger, then repeat. Be sure to name your shapes so you can call them.

Remember how to set up an animation? Talk to a particular turtle, set your list of shapes with **setsh**, and then make repeated calls to forward. For an animation that isn't really moving, the turtle can move forward by a tiny amount each time, such as 0.01 turtle step (that's one one-hundredth of a turtle step).

Now you need to change **win** so it announces "You win," calls **Page2**, talks to a list of turtles (in brackets), sets shapes, and repeats a command to go forward a tiny amount. Test your new **win** by typing **win** in the Command Center from Page1. Does it work?

Now be sure to adjust **setup** so that it goes back to **Page1** to start the game over.

One more thing: the users need some directions. On **Page1** you can add a text box that says something like "This is a two-player racing game. Answer questions to win!"

Play your game! Use the Presentation Mode under the Gadgets menu. (To get out of Presentation Mode, click on the black surrounding area.)

#14 Hangman I: Going Loopy

Now we are going to learn how to make loops. A loop repeats the same set of steps over and over, until an ending condition is met. Loops are common to all computer languages, and it's time we learned about them! We'll need to know about loops for this game, Hangman. This is a game that

- asks a user for a letter, and

- evaluates it to see if it is one of the letters we had chosen.

Then it does those again and again. That's a loop, all right!

Here is a flow chart of a simple loop:

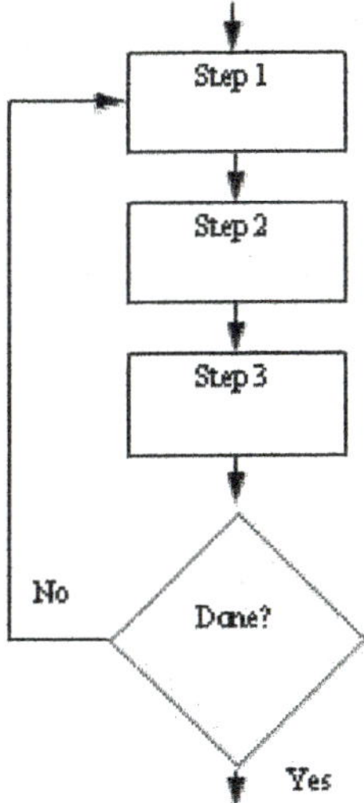

Notice the steps that follow each other down the page. Then comes the decision diamond. If we are done, we go on. If we are not done, we go back to Step 1.

We've actually used loops before: **repeat** is a simple loop, for example. We could say

repeat 6 [lots of steps]

That would be a loop that repeats six times. We could use **repeat** and end the Hangman loop when the user has guessed six times. But that won't do—we need to end the loop when the user has guessed six *wrong* answers. We have some more to learn.

Our loop needs to count only the wrong guesses, stopping the loop at six. We will need what is called a *counter* in our loop. A counter is another universal element in computer languages. We create a variable called **counter** and set its value to 0. We go through the series of steps, and at the end of the series we add 1 to what's in the variable **counter**. Then we go through the series of steps again, and add 1 to the counter again. When the counter equals six, we stop. This is called an **incremented loop**. (Incrementing is going step-by-step.) There are various ways to set one up in Logo.

In most computer languages, the code for incrementing at the end of the loop looks something like this:

:counter = :counter + 1

If you have had any algebra, you might think this means something like

x = x + 1

Here, x is a math variable that stands for any number. If you substitute 10 for x, you get 10 equals 10 plus 1. We all know that's silly! But in computer languages statements like that are common. Can you figure out why?

It's because of the nature of computer variables—they are nothing more than storage places. So you look at the right-hand side of the statement first. You take the value stored in **counter**, add one to it, and put the number back into storage. It's really not that strange after all. Let's take a look at that line again:

:counter = :counter + 1

It means this: Add 1 to the value in **counter**, and then store it again in the storage spot called **counter**.

Now, Logo has some quirks, and here is one! That line of code won't work. We have to use this line of code instead:

make "counter sum :counter 1

Can you see that it means the same thing? Let's draw a picture of a loop with a counter:

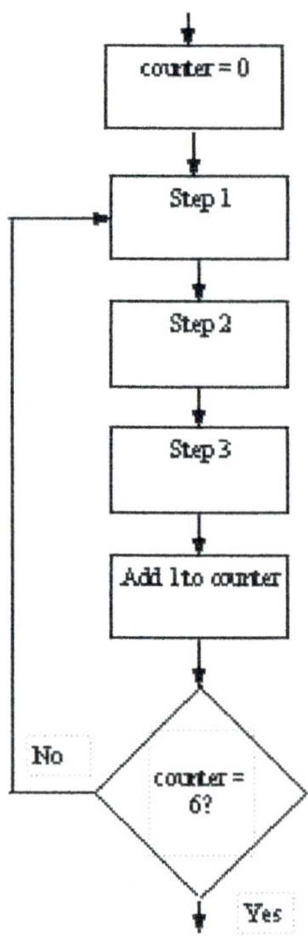

Let's make some test code. Open a new file and type this into your Procedures Page:

```
to Main
  local "counter
  make "counter 0
  talkto "t1
  forward 15 wait 1 ;step 1
  right 90;step 2
  forward 15 wait 1 ;step 3
  make "counter sum :counter 1
end


to Start
  Main
end
```

Now, go to the Procedures Page and make a **Start** button. What do you think will happen when we push it? Go ahead and do it.

I hope you weren't expecting a loop, because we didn't make one! Our code just follows a sequence of steps and then ends. We need to make an adjustment to get it to loop.

Our loop has to have some code to make it loop, and also an exit condition. Let's work on the loop part first. Go to the Help vocabulary and type in **loop**. What do you see? Nothing! We need another idea. How about using **launch**? That starts up a process that keeps repeating itself until we stop. That sounds like the definition of a loop!

Here's what the help vocabulary says about **launch**:

launch word-or-list-to-run

*Runs the input as an independent parallel process. If the process is launched from the Command Center, the cursor reappears immediately. Use **cancel,** the Cancel menu item, the Stop All menu item, or Ctrl+Break to stop the process. See also **forever**.*

Let's look up **forever**, too:

forever word-or-list-to-run

Runs the input repeatedly as an independent parallel process. Use cancel, the Cancel menu item, the Stop All menu item, or Ctrl+Break to stop the process. See also launch.

Let's test **launch**. We'll set up our loop inside a set of brackets following **launch**. Change your **Main** code to look like this:

```
================
to Main
  local "counter
  make "counter 0
  launch
  [
    talkto "t1
    forward 15 wait 1
    right 90
    forward 15 wait 1
    make "counter sum :counter 1
  ]
end
================
to Start
  Main
end
```

Now, before we dive into an endless loop, we have to plan for a way to get out. Make a button called **stopall,** which will stop all processes. That way we can stop the action.

Go to **Page1** and push **Start**. What happens? My turtle only takes a couple of steps! Remember that when we have used **launch** before, we have included a repeat, so the code said **launch [repeat 2000[some steps]].** So we could put in **repeat 2000,** and another set of brackets.

Maybe we could use **forever** instead. Replace the word **launch** with **forever** in your **Main** code. What happens? My turtle starts making boxes and boxes! I have to press the **stopall** button to stop him. That is just what I want.

Now we have an endless loop with an exit condition, the **stopall** button. But our exit condition has nothing to do with our counter. How can we change that?

Here's an important troubleshooting idea. Let's add a marker to see what part of the program is executing. We'll add a line that say **show :counter**. When a number is printed in the Command Center, we will know that the program got as far as our marker. Add a line of code inside the loop that says **show :counter**, like this:

```
to Main
  local "counter
  make "counter 0
  forever
  [
    talkto "t1
    forward 15 wait 1
    right 90
```

```
        forward 15 wait 1
        show :counter
        make "counter sum :counter 1
    ]
end
```

Now, test it. Does a series of numbers appear in the Command Center? If not, go back and check your code against mine.

How can we stop this loop using the counter? Let's add a **when** process that looks for the number 6. To jog our memories, let's look up **when** in the Help vocabulary.

__when__ [true-or-false-instruction-list] [instruction-list]

Starts a parallel process that repeatedly tests whether the first instruction list reports true or false. If it reports true, the second instruction list is run. To stop a __when__, use cancel (only on the true-or-false-instruction-list), the Cancel menu item, the Stop All menu item, or press Ctrl+Break.

We could use **when** to continually check for the exit condition, counter equal to 6. Or we could use **if** to check once each time we go through the loop. Let's try both.

Make a **when** line that says when what's in the counter equals 6, **stopall**. (**Stopall** means stop all processes.) Where should we put it? Since it is the exit condition, let's put it just inside the loop, at the end:

```
to Main
 local "counter
 make "counter 0

 forever
 [
    talkto "t1
    forward 15 wait 1
    right 90
    forward 15 wait 1
    show :counter
    make "counter sum :counter 1
    when [:counter = 6][stopall]
 ]
end

to Start
 Main
end
```

Now, test it. Does it stop when the counter gets to 6, or do you have to press the **stopall** button?

Now, replace the **when** line with an **if** line, like this:

    if (:counter = 6) [stopall]

Remember that **if** uses parentheses instead of brackets on the condition it is checking.

Does that work too?

Exercises

1. Start with a new MicroWorlds file. Make a program separate from our example, without looking at it. This program uses **forever** to set up a two- or three-step loop. Have your turtle with pen down jump "up" and then come back down to a different spot. Use a **stopall** button to get out of the loop.

2. Create a new variable, **counter**, for this program. Set its value to 0 before the loop starts. Inside the loop, add one to the counter. Also inside the loop, add code to show the counter in the Command Center. Check to see if it works.

3. Now, hatch two new turtles on **Page1**. If the counter's value is 10, **talkto** t2 and animate it as a snake to wriggle to the left across the screen. If the counter's value is 20, **talkto** t3 and animate it as a bee to fly to the right. If its value is 30, **stopall**.

4. Now, replace the **if** statements with **when** statements. Do they work? Do you know why or why not? Remember that **when** continually checks for the same thing.

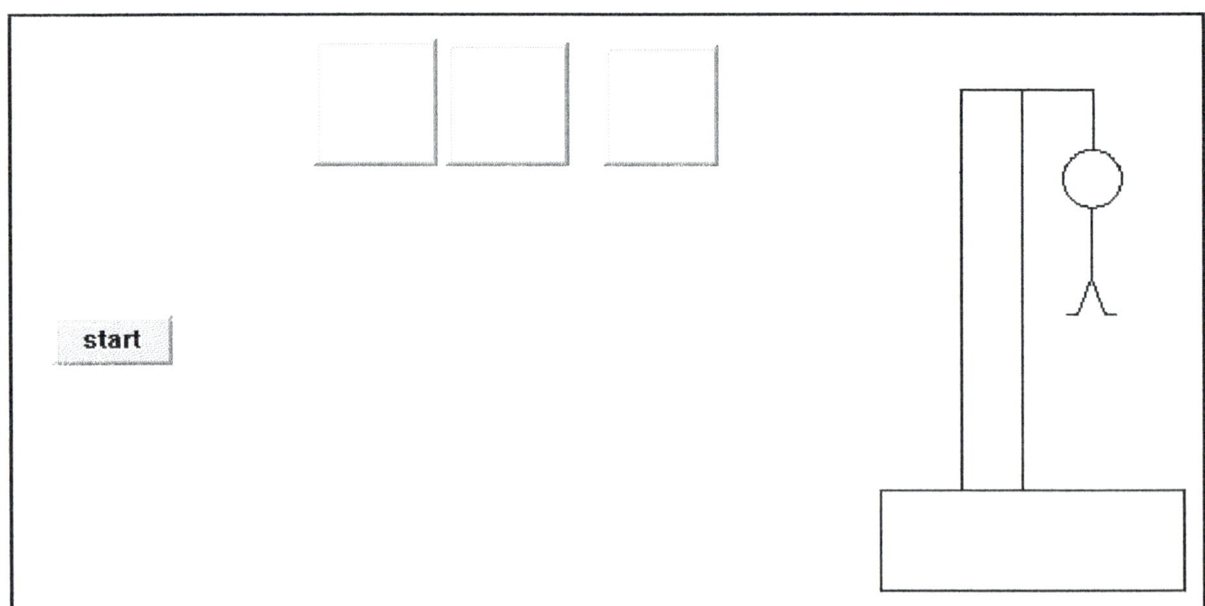

Nicole's Hangman

#15 Hangman II

(The rest of the Hangman lessons may be more advanced than a middle-school student would like. If so, please feel free to skip them and go on to the next game, City.)

Now, how can we apply what we have learned to Hangman?

In Hangman, the user has six tries to guess the letters in a word. When a guess is wrong, the computer draws a piece of a hanging man. After six wrong guesses, the man is a goner.

We'll leave the drawing part till later. For now, we'll just count the wrong guesses. Let's translate this into some requirements for our first, simplified version:

- Setup: Choose a word of three or four letters for the user to guess. Set up the right number of text boxes, one for each letter in the word.

- The computer will ask the user to guess a letter.

- The computer will compare each guess to the letters chosen.

- If the letter is one of those chosen, the computer will print it in the right text box.

- If the letter is incorrect, the computer will count the wrong guess

- The computer will repeat the series of steps, beginning with asking the user to guess a letter.

- After six wrong guesses, the loop ends.

We need to replace the steps in the loop that move the turtle with steps that have to do with Hangman.

Setup

First, let's set up our Graphics Page in a new MicroWorlds file. We will set up three small text boxes on the screen to hold each letter when it is guessed. We will use the **print** command to put the letter into the text box rather than into the Command Center.

To make a text box, go to the ABC icon. Click on it, then on the graphics screen. Draw a good-sized text box, at least one inch square. It tells you that its name is **text1**. Now, using your right-hand mouse button, right click on the text box. A screen pops up that says "Show Name" is checked. Click on the box to uncheck it, and click "OK." Now the name **text1** is hidden.

Make a **Start** button. On the Procedures Page, write a procedure for **Start**.

Plan the Code

Our loop will be modeled after the loop we did in the last lesson, with the turtle moving around. Let's paste in that code from your other file for starters, and replace the three steps with Step 1, Step 2, and

Step 3. We can put a comment mark in front of Step 1, Step 2, and Step 3 to remind us that they don't really work. It should look like this:

```
to Main
  local "counter
  make "counter 0

  forever
  [
    talkto "t1
    ;Step 1
    ;Step 2
    ;Step 3
    show :counter
    make "counter sum :counter 1
    if (:counter = 6)[stopall]
  ]
end
```

What will the first step be for Hangman? Here are the loop requirements again:

The computer will ask the user to guess a letter.

The computer will compare each guess to the letters chosen.

If the letter is one of those chosen, the computer will print it in the right text box.

If the letter is incorrect, the computer will count the wrong guess.

It looks like the first box inside the loop will be one asking the user to guess a letter.

Can you make a sketch of all the boxes in a diagram of our Hangman loop? Write the instructions in pseudocode for now. Don't turn the page until you do.

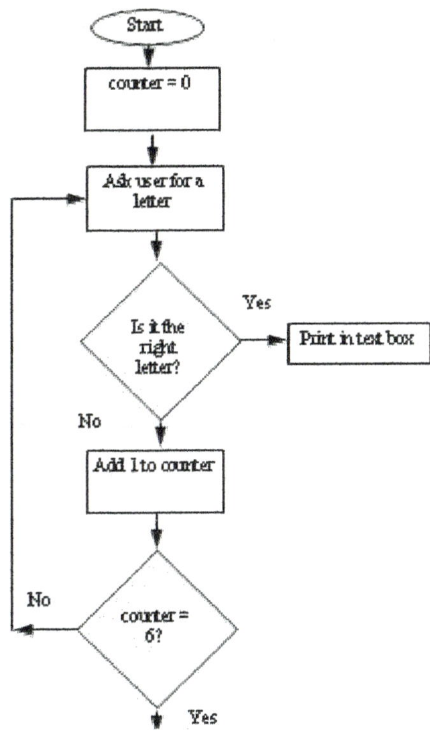

Here's a sketch to start with. You see that inside the loop the program asks for a letter and then evaluates it. If it is the right letter, it prints it in a text box. If it isn't, it adds one to the counter and goes back to the beginning of the loop, asking for a letter again.

Let's choose DOG for our hidden word. From our diagram, here is some pseudocode for the loop steps:

> **;ask the user for a letter**
> **;if the answer is a d, print it in a text box**
> **;if the answer is an o, print it in a text box**
> **;if the answer is a g, print it in a text box**
> **;otherwise, add one to the counter**
> **;if the counter = 6, stop the loop.**

Sandboxing

Now, we need to do some sandboxing.

What tools do we need? We want to ask for a letter from the user, test it, and print it in the text box.

Remember **question**? Look it up in the Help vocabulary. Look up **answer**, too. Now, look up **print,** to jog your memory.

If we just tell it to **print** the letter and have only one text box, the letters might end up out of order. That's why we need three different little text boxes. We'll tell the computer to put a d in **text1**, an o in **text2**, or a g in **text3**. Here's how we differentiate: we **talkto** the text boxes, the way we **talkto** turtles. So we **talkto "text1**, and so on.

Come up with some Logo code for the steps inside the loop. Type your loop steps into **Main**, replacing Step 1, Step 2, and Step 3. Work on it for a while before you turn the page and look at my code.

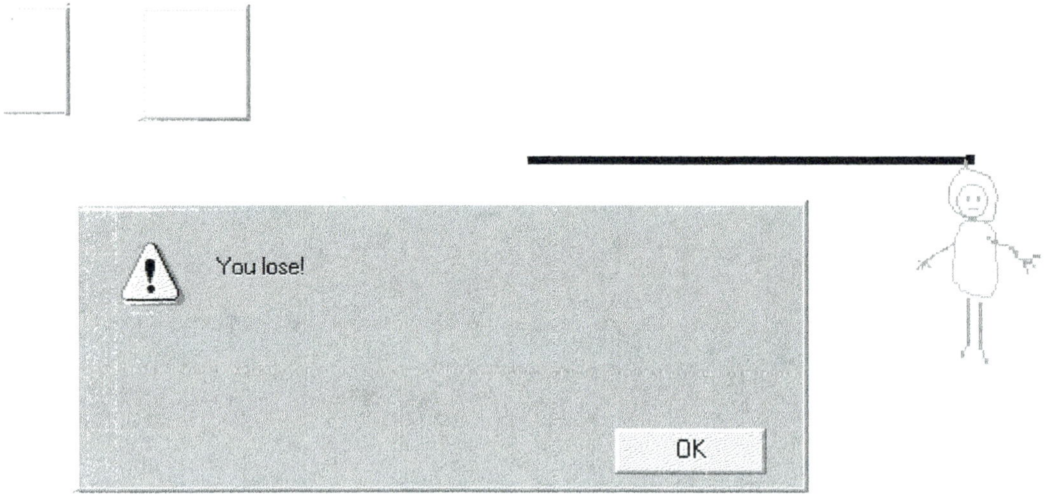

My Hangman

After you click "OK," eyes close.

Here is mine:

```
to Main
  local "counter
  make "counter 0

  forever
  [
   question [Please give me a letter]
   if (answer = "d) [talkto "text1 print answer]
   if (answer = "o) [talkto "text2 print answer]
   if (answer = "g) [talkto "text3 print answer]
   show :counter
   make "counter sum :counter 1
   if (:counter = 6)[stopall]
  ]
end

to Start
  Main
end
```

Test your creation.

Hmm, mine is counting all the answers, not just the wrong ones! I forgot to put something in to account for "otherwise" add one to the counter. Hmm. We need to change our line that adds one to the counter, using this logic:

;if it's not d, o , or g, add one to the counter.

Back to the Sandbox for Some Logic!

We need to construct a statement that means "it's not d, o, or g," that will be either true or false. So we need to look at these logical operators: **and**, **not**, and **or.**

Let's consider this Boolean statement (statement that is either true or false):

It is raining.

Let's use it like this:

If (it is raining) [take my umbrella].

If the Boolean statement in parentheses evaluates to true, then we take the action that follows. If it evaluates to false, we don't.

How about this?

If (it is raining) and (I have to go out)[take the umbrella].

Now the **and** is linking two Boolean statements. If *both* Boolean statements are true, then the compound statement is true, and we take the action following. Sounds kind of obvious, doesn't it?

What if I replaced **and** with **or**? Then only one of the Boolean statements, or conditions, needs to be true for the compound statement to evaluate to true, so we take the following action.

If (it is raining) or (I have to go out)[take the umbrella].

We can see that **or** isn't the right operator to use here. It doesn't make sense. But we could use **or** in a different sentence.

If (it is raining) or (the weatherman says it will rain) [take the umbrella].

Here if either of these conditions is true, the compound statement is true, and so we take the following action. That is the nature of the **or** operator: only one of the conditions has to be true.

Let's go over that again. Is this compound statement true or false?

(it is raining) and (I have to go out)

It's true if both of the conditions in parentheses are true, and otherwise it is false.

Using **or**,

(it is raining) or (I have to go out)

the linked statement is true if one of the conditions in parentheses is true.

Why are we so interested in whether it evaluates to true or false? Because when we use **when** and **if**, in Logo, we have to have a condition that evaluates to true or false. Specifically, we want a condition that looks something like this:

If (answer = "d or answer = "o or answer = "g) [add one to the counter]

Oops! In this case, if one of those small statements is true, we add one to the counter. That's not what we want at all! We want to add one to the counter if the answer is NOT d, o, or g! What do we do?

There's another logical operator called **not**. It simply changes a condition's true evaluation to false, and vice versa. So what we really want is this:

If not (answer = "d or answer = "o or answer = "g) [add one to the counter]

You may think this logic is pretty strange. It's like speaking English, kind of. But you have to use your logical brain powers to make sense of it. Don't pooh-pooh it though! Logic is very important for programmers. This logic stuff is just the way computers think!

Now, back to the line above. Of course, I am writing in pseudocode, so it isn't really Logo yet. How are we going to translate it to Logo?

Here's what Help says about **not**:

> ***not***
>
> ***not*** *true-or-false*
>
> *Reports the logical inverse of its input. See **and** and **or**.*
>
> *Example:*
>
> *show empty? [ ]*
>
> *true*
>
> *show not empty? [ ]*
>
> *false*

In other words, the input for **not** is a condition that evaluates to true or false, and no parentheses are needed. It's pretty much like *not* in English.

But **or** isn't like *or* in English. Here's what help says about **or**:

> ***or***
>
> ***or*** *true-or-false1 true-or-false2*
>
> *(**or** true-or-false1 true-or-false2 true-or-false3...)*
>
> *Reports true if any of its inputs report true. If more than two inputs are used, **or** and its inputs must be enclosed in parentheses. See **and** and **not**.*
>
> *Examples:*
>
> *show or (2 = 2) (3 = 5)*
>
> *true*
>
> *show (or (2 = 2) (3 = 5) (8 = 9))*
>
> *true*

In other words, since we have three inputs concerning d, o, and g, we need to use parentheses as in the second example. Here is our rough code again:

If not (answer = "d or answer = "o or answer = "g) [add one to the counter]

Let's use **(or ...)** and see what happens:

If not (or answer = "d answer = "o answer = "g) [add one to the counter]

One more thing we have to do: change the second part to Logo.

make "counter sum :counter 1

Put this line in your code and see what happens!

If not (or answer = "d answer = "o answer = "g) [make "counter sum :counter 1]

Does it count only the wrong answers now? It should.

Exercises

Tell whether these compound statements are true or false:

1. Dogs like walks **and** trees can swim.

2. Dogs like walks **or** trees can swim.

3. Not (dogs like walks **and** trees can swim).

4. Not (dogs like walks **or** trees can swim).

#16 Hangman III

Here's a recap of the requirements we have covered so far in our Hangman game:

- Setup: Choose a word of three or four letters for the user to guess. Set up the right number of text boxes, one for each letter in the word.

- The computer will ask the user to guess a letter.

- The computer will compare each guess to the letters chosen.

- If the letter is one of those chosen, the computer will print it in the right text box.

- If the letter is incorrect, the computer will count the wrong guess

- The computer will repeat the series of steps, beginning with asking the user to guess a letter.

- After six wrong guesses, the loop ends.

Here's another set of requirements for us to take up now:

- After six wrong guesses, the computer announces "You lose! The word was __________." The game ends.

- If the user guesses all the letters correctly, the computer announces "You win!" and ends the game.

First, let's make a diagram of our game with these two exit conditions.

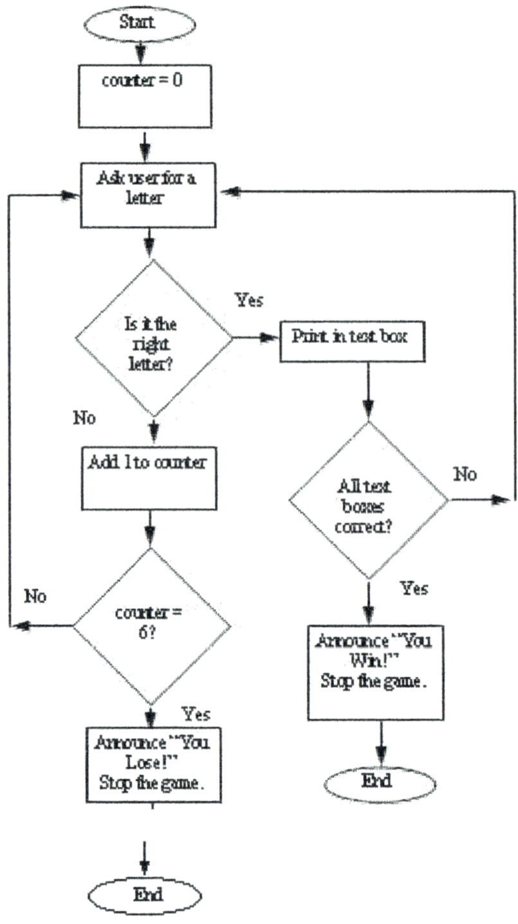

You see that I have drawn the two exit conditions (losing and winning) as parallel, independent processes. That's why there are two separate paths coming down the page. We will work on the "you lose" condition first.

First, we need to come up with a line of code that does what the "announce you lose" diagram box says. Think about it and write it down on scratch paper. You will need to use **announce** and **stopall**.

Now, we need to figure out where to put the new line of code. Here is our Main from the last lesson:

```
to Main
 local "counter
 make "counter 0
 forever
 [
 question [Please give me a letter]
 if (answer = "d) [talkto "text1 print answer]
 if (answer = "o) [talkto "text2 print answer]
 if (answer = "g) [talkto "text3 print answer]
```

```
    show :counter
    if not ( or answer = "d answer = "o answer = "g) [make "counter sum :counter 1]
    if (:counter = 6)[stopall]
    ]
end
```

Do you see the line we need to change? It's this one:

if (:counter = 6)[stopall]

Let's change it to this:

if (:counter = 6)[announce [You lose!] stopall]

Does that work? It should. Or sort of, anyway. Now my game is telling me that I lost even though I guessed the right answers! What I need is the other exit condition operating.

Let's look at the diagram again for that one. It says, in pseudocode,

;if all text boxes are correct, announce you win, and stop the game.

Let's go ahead and insert that pseudocode, just inside the loop at the end.

But how does the computer tell if all the boxes are correctly filled? What ideas do you have? Think about it for a minute.

Here's one way: we could create variables to hold the correct responses, and fill them as we fill the text boxes. Then we could check the variables to see if their contents are correct. Then we would stop the loop. (There's another way that involves using the text boxes as sort-of variables, with their own odd set of commands, but that doesn't transfer to other languages very well so we won't use it.)

We can create the variables in the same line where we created **counter**. How about this:

local [counter letter1 letter2 letter3]

If the answer is **d**, we want to print the **d** in the text box and *also* put the **d** in the variable **letter1**. If the answer is **o**, we want to print the **o** in the text box and *also* put the **o** in the variable **letter2**. Same with **g**, for **letter3**. Can you see how to do this? Try it yourself and see if it works. Then turn the page to see mine.

I changed loop steps to look like this:

```
to Main
  local [counter letter1 letter2 letter3]
  make "counter 0
  forever
  [
    question [Please give me a letter]
    if (answer = "d) [talkto "text1 print answer make "letter1 answer]
    if (answer = "o) [talkto "text2 print answer make "letter2 answer]
    if (answer = "g) [talkto "text3 print answer make "letter3 answer]
    show :counter
    if not ( or answer = "d answer = "o answer = "g) [make "counter sum :counter 1]
    if (:counter = 6)[announce [You lose!] stopall]
    ;if all text boxes are correct, announce you win, and stop the game.
  ]
end
```

Now that the variables are filling up nicely, how do we check that the contents are correct? Let's use this simple line of reasoning. If **letter1** contains **d** and **letter2** contains **o** and **letter3** contains **g**, then announce "You win" and stop the game. The key word here is **and**. Remember its special use from the lesson on logic? I will jog your memory.

If (it is raining) and (I have to go out)[take the umbrella].

Now the **and** is linking two Boolean statements. If *both* Boolean statements are true, then we take the action following.

What if I use **or**? Then only one of the Boolean statements needs to be true.

If (it is raining) or (the weatherman says it will rain) [take the umbrella].

Let's go back to our hangman problem.

We want to say

;if all text boxes are correct, announce you win, and stop the game.

Actually, we want to use the variable names letter1, letter2, and letter3 to say something more like this:

;if ([letter1 contains d] and [letter2 contains o] and [letter3 contains g])
**   [announce you win and stop the game]**

First, let's look first at the simple statements. How will we translate [letter1 contains d] to Logo?

The equals sign is a Boolean (true-false) operator in Logo. A statement using = is a Boolean statement, evaluating to true or false. So let's try using =, with a space before and after. Will this work?

> **letter1 = d**

We need say "what's in" letter1, not the name of the variable, so we will use the dots operator :
> **:letter1 = d**

But the computer probably will try to read **d** as a procedure or action, not as a name, so we had better put quotes in front of it. Let's try
> **:letter1 = "d**

We should be able to construct the simple statements from that example. Now, let's look up **and** again in the MicroWorlds Help.

> ***and***
>
> ***and*** *true-or-false1 true-or-false2*
>
> *(**and** true-or-false1 true-or-false2 true-or-false3...)*
>
> *Reports true if all its inputs report true. If more than two inputs are used, **and** and its inputs must be enclosed in parentheses. See **or** and **not**.*
>
> *Example:*
>
> *show (and 2 = 2 5 = 5 6 = 6)*
>
> *true*

We can see that **and**, like other MicroWorlds procedures, is followed by its inputs, separated by spaces. If there are more than two inputs, we need to enclose **and** with the inputs in parentheses.

Now, let's see if you can use this information to cast this pseudocode into Logo:

> **;if ([letter1 contains d] and [letter2 contains o] and [letter3 contains g])[announce you win and stop the game]**

Work on it and test it.

Exercises

1. Make a **reset** procedure that is called at the beginning of the game, so that the user can play the game again and again, and have the text boxes cleared by pressing **Start** to start the game. Look up **cleartext** in the Help vocabulary and use it.

2. Change the guessed word to a longer word with different letters. Remember to use **copy** and **paste**, and then make changes, to reduce the amount you have to retype.

3. Extra credit: Consider this problem: Create code that rejects the "right" letters if they are used more than once. How would you solve it? Create pseudocode for key lines. Cast into Logo.

#17 Hangman IV

Here's our next requirement:

Make a six-piece drawing that adds a piece of a hanging man each time the user makes a wrong guess. Use hidden turtles for each piece of the man (**ht** means hide turtle; **st** means show turtle).

First, go to the shape center and make six shapes that will make up a hanging man. You can name them like this: noose, head, body, arm1, arm2, legs.

Now, on your Page1, use the drawing tools to draw a bar that the noose will hang from. Hatch five more turtles. Put the shapes on them in order: noose on **t1**, head on **t2**, body on **t3**, and so on. Collect them so that they make a drawing of a hanging man. Change the drawings if you need to make them match up. Be sure to put the drawing off to the side of the page, where it won't be covered by the question/announcement box in the middle.

From Hannah's Hangman: Hanging in Progress

What we want to do is at the beginning hide the turtles that make up the drawing, and show them one by one as the counter number increases. Can you think of a way to do that? Think about it before you turn the page.

Here's what we can do: At the beginning of the code, just after the list of variables, talk to a list of all the turtles, and then command **ht** for hide turtle.

Lower down in the program, inside the loop near the end, we will make a set of **if** statements, meaning:

;if the counter equals 1, talk to t1, show the turtle, and set its shape to noose.

Can you translate that to Logo?

Exercises

1. Make another shape that shows the hanging man is a goner (eyes are x's for instance). Change to that shape after the computer announces "You lose!"

2. Make a separate procedure called **win**. In the winning case, hide all but one of the turtles. For the one still showing, change the shape to something fun, like a fireball. Animate it.

Hannah's Hangman Is a Goner!

#18 City I

This is a game that asks the user for directions and then draws a busy street, lined with houses and full of animated characters zipping back and forth. Or it could be a variation on this; one student drew an army camp of barracks with jeeps, trucks, and airplanes moving through and above it, complete with blinking lights. Use your imagination when you plan your city! Here are two examples:

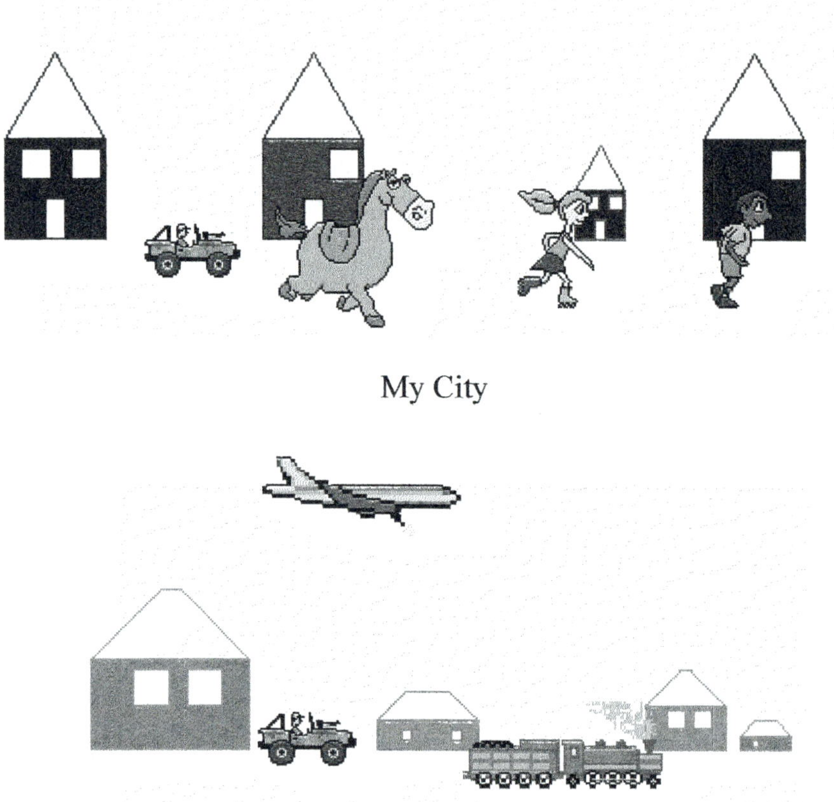

My City

Paul's Army Camp

Here is the plan:

- The user presses the **Start** button.

- The drawing turtle moves to the left edge of the screen, near the bottom so the question boxes won't cover up the houses it draws.

- The computer says to the user, "I will build you a house. Do you want big or small? (type big or small)"

- The turtle, **t1**, draws a house, sized either big or small. The houses are identical except for size.

- It waits a bit so the user can see the drawing.

- The computer asks, "Do you want 1 or 2 windows?"

- T1 draws one or two windows. It waits a bit.

- The computer asks, "Do you want a red or blue house?"

- T1 colors the house in with red or blue (or two other colors you choose). Now the house is built. It moves to the right some steps.

- The computer asks, "Do you want another house? Y or N"

- If the user answers "Y," the loop starts over. We could end up with a street lined with houses.

- After the city is drawn, the program launches at least three animations walking or flying down the street (across the screen).

- The user can stop the animations and start over by pressing **Start**.

There are two things about this program I want you to notice right off the bat. One is that it contains a loop. It repeats a set of steps over and over. The other is that it uses variables. The **house** procedure will use a variable sent from **Main** to determine what size to draw the house.

I want you to take out a pencil and paper and work on a flow chart for this program. Don't turn the page to look at mine until you have worked on it for 10 minutes. Hint: it looks a lot like the one for Race.

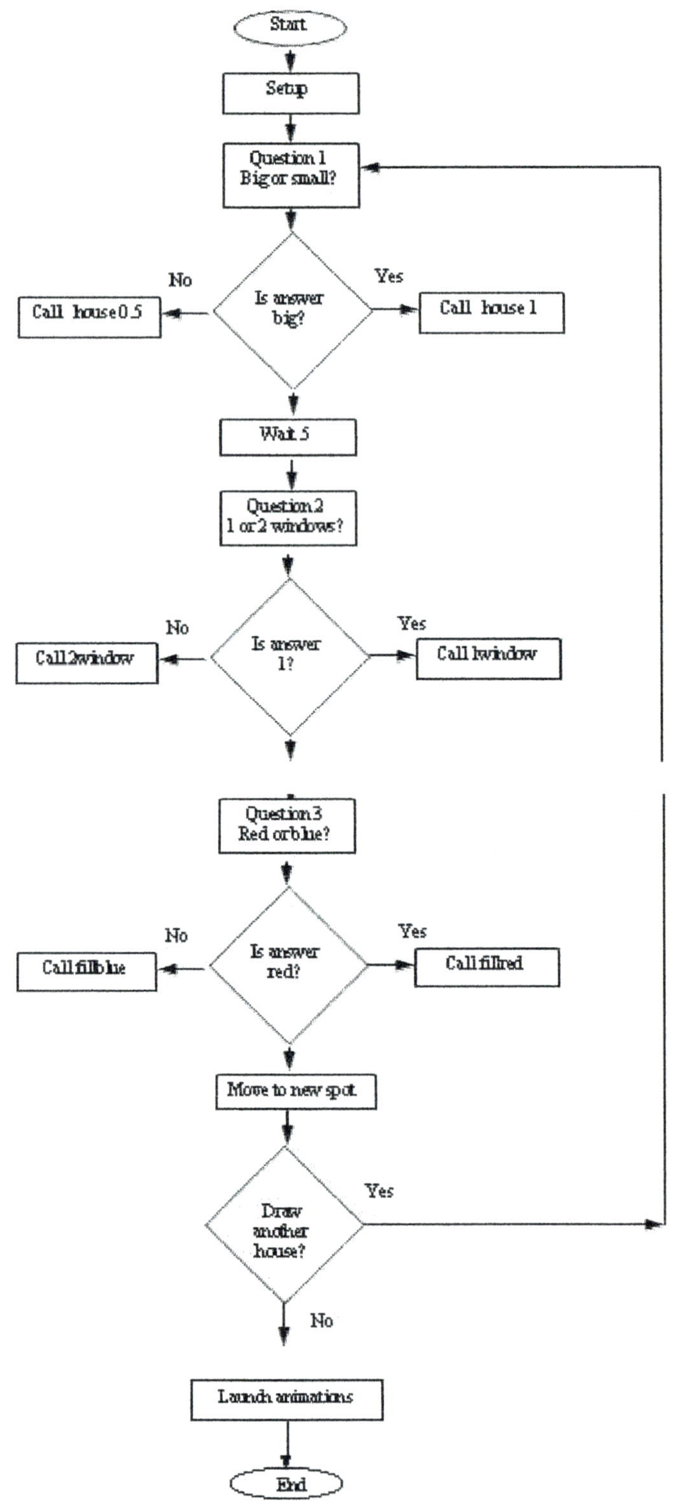

Flow Chart for City

96

First, let's consider what code we will use to make our loop. We will have a bunch of steps, and at the end of the steps, we will get input from the user on whether to loop or not. We could pattern our loop after our Hangman loop, using **forever** to start it, and stopping it with an **if** statement at the end. For example, we can ask the user if he wants to continue, Y or N.

;if the answer is N, animate, wait a while, and stop the action.

Notice that that is not Logo, but pseudocode, so we put a semicolon in front of it.

Here's another way to do it: don't use **forever** at the top; just start the steps in the loop. Then at the end of the loop, ask the user if he or she wants to continue, Y or N. If the answer is Y, we call **Main**. If it is N, we don't. So we are calling **Main** from within **Main**. Sound strange? It works, as long as you have a way to get out of the loop. The problem here is that the first line of our Main is **setup**, but we don't want to run **setup** every time we go through the loop. We would have to move **setup** out of **Main** and into the **Start** button procedure. So **Start** would look like this:

to Start
  cg
  setup
  Main
end

The advantage of this plan is that we don't have to stop all the action to get out of the loop. So the animations can just keep chugging along until the user presses the **Start** button or closes the window. We could add a **stopall** button too.

So, which loop shall we use? Let's use the one that calls **Main** from **Main**. We could use practice with that one. Now our flow chart for **Main** looks a little different at the top:

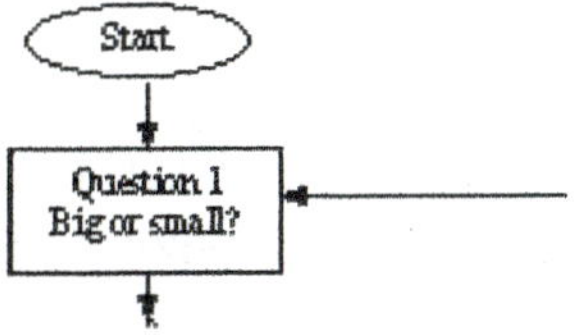

Next, let's brush up on variables a little. Remember that variables are storage places, like pigeonhole mailboxes. A first line for a procedure can create a variable storage place, like this:

to house :size

Here **house** is the name of the procedure, and **size** is the name of the variable used inside the procedure. So, now the procedure **house** needs one input. When we call this procedure **house** from **Main**, we need to send it an input to go into the variable **size**. So our command from **Main** would look like this:

house 1

for the full-sized house, or

house 0.5

for the half-sized house. Now, inside the procedure **house**, we will use this number that **Main** sent over. Instead of **forward 1**, we can say **forward :size**. This means "go forward by what's in **size**." We're reading those two dots in front of **size** as "what's in." We will worry about the details of **house** in a minute.

Now, using the flowchart, code your **Main** procedure. Use **question, answer,** and **if** statements. Brush up on those by looking at the Help vocabulary if you need to. Remember to create the loop by calling **Main** at the end, like this:

ifelse (answer = "y)[Main][animate]

In the middle of **Main** we need a line that moves the turtle to a new spot to draw a new house. Let's consider that line. First pick the pen up. Then we need to drop the turtle down from the windowsill to the street level, and then move it to the right. To drop it to street level, you could make use of the built-in procedure **sety**. If you command **sety –120**, the turtle will drop up or down from wherever it is, to the level of Y= -120. Try it: type **sety –120** in the Command Center, and see where your turtle goes. If this isn't where your street level is, put the turtle at your street level and type **show pos** in the Command Center. It will give you two numbers, the x and Ycoordinates. Take the second one; that's your Ycoordinate. Now test **sety** with that number. After dropping the turtle to street level, move it to the right 100 or 125 turtle steps. Add a comment to remind you what is going on, like this: **;moving the turtle to a new spot.**

To get our program going, we need to code something for these procedures: **setup, house** with one input, **1window, 2window, fillred, fillblue,** and **animate**. I already gave you **Start**.

To code **setup**, put your turtle where you want it to start, using the mouse. This will be along the left side of the Graphics Page, fairly low. Now use **show pos** in the Command Center to find its coordinates. In the **setup** procedure, tell **t1** to set its position there.

How do we code **house**? This is actually from *Computer Science Pure and Simple Book 1*, where we drew a house and then added a variable that re-sized it. First, don't worry now about the variable use inside the procedure. Make a procedure **to house :size** that draws a house but doesn't actually use **size** yet. It can be a simple house, or a more complex one. A simple house is a square 50 turtle steps on a side, a triangle on top of it, and a door. Remember that if the turtle is drawing a triangle with equal sides, it turns 120 degrees at each corner.

Next we will make two window procedures, **1window** and **2window.** One draws one window, one draws two. Each one starts from the spot where the drawing of **house** ended. Make a little sketch with dimensions on it, to tell your turtle where to go to start a window.

Next, we will make two procedures, **fillred** and **fillblue**. In each one, the turtle picks its pen up (**pu**) and then takes a step or two into the square that represents the side of the house. It sets the color in the bucket using **setc**; for example, **setc 15** sets it to red, and **setc 105** sets it to blue. It puts its pen down (**pd**). Then it fills the side of the house with color using **fill**.

Animate is a fancy procedure we will develop later. For the time being, just make a dummy:

to animate
end

This will show us if our program as a whole works.

Make a **Start** button.

So, at the moment, we have a program that loops using a call to **Main** at the end of the loop. It draws houses that are the same size, with different colors, with different numbers of windows. The animation planned for the end isn't in place yet, and neither is the house re-size. Test it and tinker with it until it works!

Exercise

After you get the simplified program to work using the call to **Main** at the end of the loop (called a recursive call to **Main**), save your work. Now save it again in a different file, and see if you can get the program to loop using **forever**. Put **forever** at the top of the series of steps in **Main**, with brackets [and] around the steps. You will need to change two more things to provide a way to stop the loop. These are the line at the end of the loop that begins with **if** and provides a way out of the loop, and the procedure **animate**. You will need to put the command **stopall** inside the animate procedure. If you find your program stuck in an infinite loop, press **control-alt-delete** keys at the same time to bring up a menu that allows you to shut down the MicroWorlds application and try again. Then put this exercise aside; it isn't the program we will move forward with in the next lesson.

Stephen's City. The characters animate.

#19 City II

We are moving forward with the version of **Main** from the last lesson in which **Main** calls itself in order to create a loop. In order to finish our program, we need to flesh out the two procedures **house** and **animate.** In this lesson we will work on **house**.

Here is our requirement: add a variable to **house**, and change the line in **Main** that calls **house** to add a variable input.

We need to re-size **house**. First, let's jog our memories again on what we learned about variables. Remember that a variable for a computer is a storage spot, like one of a lot of cubbyholes or mailboxes set up in the computer's RAM, or temporary memory. We have created a variable named **size** in our house procedure. We are going to take the user's input, *big* or *small*. If it's *big*, we will send the number 1 over from **Main** as the input to **house** to be stored in **size**. If it's *small*, we'll send over the number 0.5. Here's what the sending looks like:

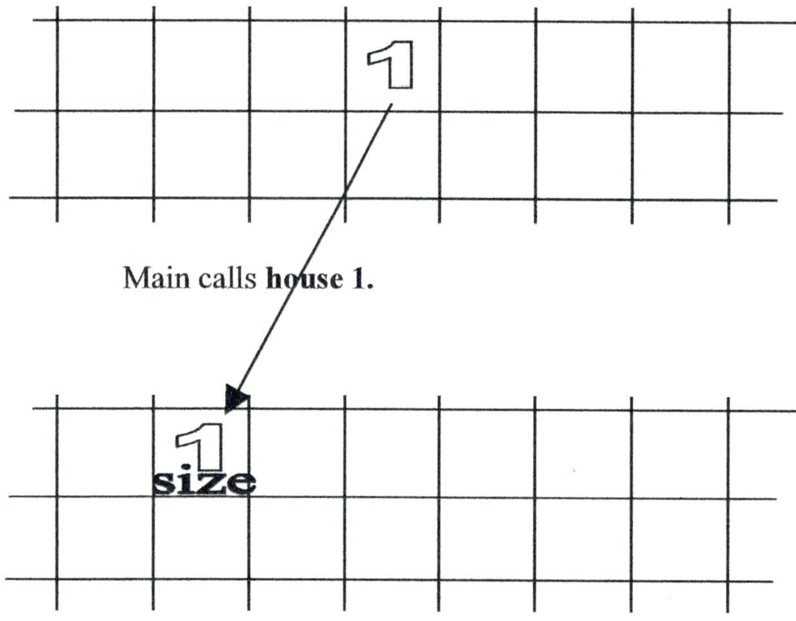

Main calls **house 1.**

In **house**, **:size** stores the 1.

So, inside of our **house** procedure, what do we do with what's in this variable **size**? We are going to multiply all the lengths in the house drawing by it. So if **size** contains 1, we get a house 50 turtle steps wide. If it contains 0.5, we get one that is 25 turtle steps wide.

In your **house** procedure, find all the places the turtle goes forward a number, say **forward 50**. Change that to say **forward 50 * :size**. Remember that * is computer-ese for multiplication, and **:size** means "what's in size." Use copy and paste to drop the * **:size** in the right places. Don't change the angle inputs, though, where the turtle is turning right or left. Don't change the turtle headings. Now, test your program. Does it resize the house if you ask for a small house?

Oops! We'll need to resize the windows too! We need to draw big windows or small windows, depending on whether the user chose *big* or *small*.

For starters, let's do the same thing as before, and create an input variable for **1window** and **2window**; in other words, from **Main** we'll call these procedures using **1window 1** or **1window 0.5**. Make your changes to the code for **1window** and **2window**—add a variable to the first line of the procedure, such as **w1size** and **w2size**. Inside the procedures, multiply every call to forward by **what's in w1size** or **what's in w2size**, such as :

> **forward 10 * :w1size**

Now, take a look at our **Main** code.

> **question [I will build you a house. Do you want big or small?]**
> **ifelse (answer = "big) [house 1][house 0.5]**

The second line, you recall, means that if the answer is big, call **house** 1; otherwise, call **house** 0.5. OK, that part works great. Here we have input from the user and use it to choose whether to build a big house or a small house. Next:

> **question [Do you want 1 or 2 windows?]**
> **ifelse (answer = 1) [1window][2window]**

Oops, we have a problem! Here, we have more input from the user, this time on the number of windows. We have now lost the input about big or small house—it isn't stored anywhere. So if we want to make a change to draw a big or small window, we don't know which!

Think about how to solve this problem. You're an experienced programmer now, and you should be able to come up with a solution before you turn the page!

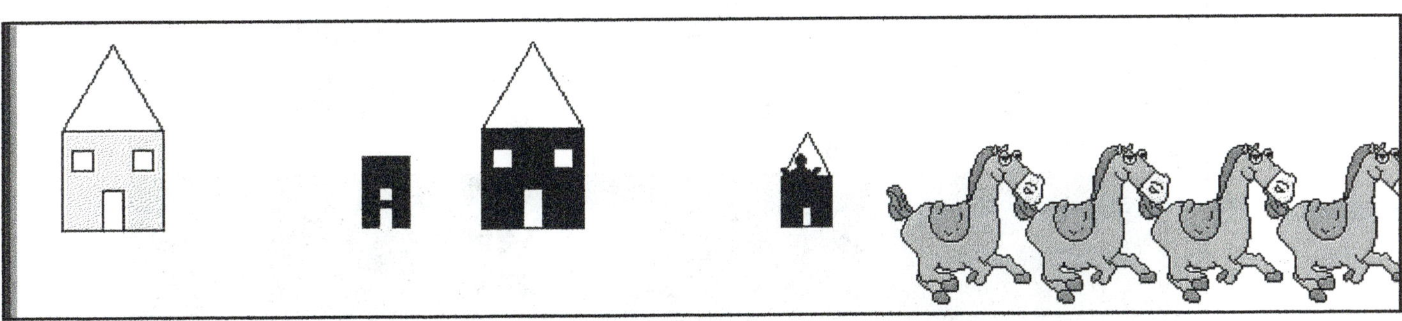

Lianna's City

We need to create a variable to store the size indicated by the user long enough to use it in the calls to **1window** and **2window**. This variable will be *local* to **Main.** (A local variable is one that is not usable in another procedure. One which is usable in all procedures is a *global* variable. This is poor programming practice, with plenty of room for bugs.) Since programmers generally declare all variables at the top of a procedure, insert a first line in **Main** that creates a local variable called **hsize**. Look up the procedure **local** in the Help vocabulary before you do it.

Now, where will you use **hsize**? You need to store the user's preference in it. In the line that says

    ifelse (answer = "big) [house 1][house 0.5]

you will need to add to the stuff in the brackets, so that

    ;if the answer is big, call house with input 1 and make what's in hsize 1
    ;otherwise call house with input 0.5 and make what's in hsize 0.5.

Can you translate that pseudocode to Logo? Look up **make** in the help vocabulary to make sure you are using it right.

Also use **hsize** to:

- re-size the windows and

- resize the distance in **Main** that moves the turtle down the street before it starts to draw again.

Get this to work by the beginning of the next class.

Crystal's City

#20 City III

Your City project should be working well now, except for the animations. Hatch four more turtles.

Let's write our animation for **t2**. Remember, this is how we set up an animation:

- Talk to that turtle. Show turtle (**st**); set heading (**seth**).

- Using setshape, or **setsh,** we give a list of shapes for a turtle to take, one after the other, for example, **setsh [horse1 horse2].**

- Next, we set up a situation that repeatedly calls **forward**. Each time **forward** is called, a new shape is used. For example, **repeat 10 [forward 3].**

- Next, put in a pause to make the action more realistic. Use **wait.** For example, **repeat 10 [forward 3 wait 1].**

Doctor up the shapes in the shape center (be sure to scroll down to see them all) or create your own. To create a shape, double click on a shape or on a shape blank, and use the drawing tools. Be sure you give them unique names. You can use two or three as an action sequence. Here's how to copy a shape that exists in order to paste it onto another shape and change it slightly: select the shape in the shape center (you see a square around it). Hit **control-c** to copy it to the clipboard. Now select a shape blank. You see a square around it. Hit **control-v** to paste the shape there. Double click on it now to make your changes. You can change the shape's color using the fill bucket or a very fat line. If you are drawing a vehicle, make its lights blink or change color as it moves.

Now, to get each animation to work as an independent process, use **launch. Launch** works with **repeat**, like this:

> **talkto "t2**
> **launch [repeat 5000 [forward 3 wait 1]]**

One more thing: we need to adjust **setup** to take into account the animating turtles. Add some lines to setup that do this:

> **;talk to t2, t3, t4 and t5,**
> **;pull pen up, hide turtle**
> **;set position at some starting point in your street. All these turtles can start at the same point.**

And, don't forget to show turtle (**st**) in the **animate** procedure.

By the beginning of next class, get the animations to work, and finish the game. Draw a background, such as mountains or trees, using the drawing center tools.

Extra Credit Exercises

1. Add another option to the game. Make two house designs, and ask the user to select one. First ask if the user wants big or small, then ask the user to choose a house design, then number of windows, then color. Note: this is a complicated assignment! It is also our last Logo assignment. Are you up to it?

2. Cause night to fall as your animated characters start going across the screen. This is particularly effective if you have vehicles with blinking lights.

Tiffany's City

Paul's Army Camp, Nightfall

Part II: Internet Exercises

#21 Internet Scavenger Hunt: Animals

Let's talk a bit about what the Internet is. I hope you remember from *Book 1* our discussion about billboards: the Internet is a collection of Web sites that are like billboards in "cyberspace," or computerland. Individuals and companies pay some money to put up a billboard, or Web site, and use it to sell something, or to give out information while collecting money from advertisers.

When you are looking for information on the Internet, you need to look carefully at the Web site to judge whether the information is probably reliable. It would be easy to put up a Web site and put false or incorrect information on it. You need to look at the bottom of the Web page to see who originated it, and why. Is it a "coffee shop" selling books? Then the information is probably pretty good. Is it a political group pushing a point of view? Then whether the information is good can be more questionable. Is it an individual's personal Web site? Then beware. Also, beware of sites that have grammar and spelling errors. Individuals who are sloppy with those details will also probably be sloppy with facts.

Spyware

We also need to be very careful when cruising the Web to avoid tricks that lead you to spyware. In particular, you will often see smaller pop-up windows that want you to click on them. Some are very clever and imitate error messages that you may see on your computer. But don't click anywhere but on the upper corner x to close the window. Otherwise you may be inviting spyware contamination on your computer.

Spyware is programs that someone else downloads onto your computer to do things you probably don't want, such as continually popping little windows up asking you the same question: do you want to buy my product? (I don't know why they think that annoying the potential customer is a good way to make sales!) They may also be recording all your keystrokes (looking for credit card numbers). It is a good idea to find a free download of a spyware buster on the Internet (try download.com or look using Google). Here are some to look for: Spy Sweeper, Ad-Aware, Spybot, Easycleaner, and Spywareblaster. Once you install one or more of these, you will need to run them every few days. You will no doubt be surprised at what unknown people have already installed on your computer! Better yet, get a good software firewall like Zonealarm. This program does not replace antivirus software like Norton and McAfee, which aim at viruses coming in through email, so you should have one of those too.

Search Engine

You will probably use a search engine a lot—my favorite is Google. Before we do anything else, let's adjust Google to screen out inappropriate content. Open your browser now and type in www.google.com. Now you see the Google search screen. To the right you see **preferences**. Click on that. Scroll down to **SafeSearch Filtering**. Now choose **strict filtering**, and click **save preferences** at the bottom of the page. You land back at the search engine screen. Type in a topic you like and get a listing of sites. Now, before you click on any of the listings, read carefully. You should be able to tell if the site contains what you are interested in. Go ahead and click on one that looks likely. Can you learn something?

We are going to practice finding information on the Web using a scavenger hunt. I will give you a list of questions. Your job is to find out the answers. You should open a Word file, save it as **animal scavenger hunt answers**, and then type **1** for question one. Now, enlarge your browser, go to Google, type in exact key words—even the whole question. From the Google listing you can probably find the answer. If not, click on a likely item to go to a site to look for it. When you find the answer, copy and paste the information into the Word file. I also want you to copy and paste the URL (the address, such as http://www.Website.com) of the site where you found the answer. So your answer for question 1 might look like this:

1. Platypuses lay eggs. http://www.animalinfo.com/platypus

If you can't find an answer, skip the question and move on to the next. When you are done with the easy ones, come back and work on the harder ones. You will print the Word file to turn in to your teacher.

Internet Scavenger Hunt: Odd Facts about Animals

Rules:

- Look up the topic on the Internet using Google and find the answer to each question. Hint: use lots of keywords, or even the whole question, in your search.

- When you find the answer, paste the answer in after the question, and then paste in the URL too. If you already knew the answer, you still need to find the info on a Web page and list the URL.

- You can't use the same URL for more than one answer.

1. A cockroach can live for how long without a head?

2. A Cornish game hen is really the young of what sort of bird?

3. A female mackerel lays about how many eggs at one time?

4. A newborn kangaroo is about how long?

5. A polecat is not a cat. What is it?

6. A typical bed usually houses how many dust mites?

7. A woodpecker can peck how many times a second?

8. All clams start out as a.) males or b.) females. Which?

9. All pet hamsters are descended from a single female wild golden hamster found with a litter of 12 young in what country, what year?

10. A certain type of ant steals the larvae of other ants to keep as slaves. The slave ants build homes for and feed these ants, who cannot do anything but fight. They depend completely on their slaves for survival. What kind of ant is this?

11. An adult lion's roar can be heard about how far away?

12. Animal gestation periods—what are the shortest and the longest, and their lengths?

13. At 188 decibels, the whistle of what animal is the loudest sound produced by any animal?

14. The teeth of what animal are so sharp that Native Americans once used them as knife blades?

15. How many eyelids do camels have on each eye?

16. What lizard can move its eyes in two different directions at the same time?

17. What breed of dog was developed in Egypt about 5,000 years ago, and in the ninth century A.D. was popular with English aristocrats?

18. About how fast can dragonflies fly?

19. How long does a hen's body take to produce an egg? How long does she "rest" before her body starts making another one?

20. In its entire lifetime, a worker bee produces how much honey?

21. Baby beavers are called what?

22. It takes a lobster how long to grow to be one pound?

23. Macaroni, Gentoo, and Chinstrap are types of what animal?

24. Moles are able to tunnel how far in a day?

25. On average, pigs live for how long?

26. What shape are owl eyeballs?

27. What is the animal that never gets sick?

#22 Internet Scavenger Hunt: Geography

1. Name the two languages commonly spoken in Denmark.

2. Which dynasty of China built the Great Wall?

3. Name the spiritual leader of Tibet, now in exile.

4. What is Japan's largest lake?

5. The Great Silk Road was a merchant route linking China with what empire in the West?

6. Macao was until recently a colony of what European country?

7. What is the largest city in Kazakhstan?

8. What are the two large deserts in the southern half of central Asia?

9. What modern country was formerly known as Persia?

10. What modern country was formerly known as Babylon?

11. What three countries make up Transcaucasia?

12. What empire ruled Transcaucasia for 70 years before 1991?

13. Where did India's civilization begin?

14. Name an ancient people who built the cities of Tyre and Sidon.

15. Where was Carthage? In what modern country?

16. Who was a famous queen of Carthage?

17. Name the four large islands of Japan.

18. What is the modern name for what used to be called Burma, in Southeast Asia?

19. The official title for Thailand is Muang Thai. What does it mean?

20. Malaysia is a country spanning the Malay Peninsula and what large island?

21. What is the modern name for what Europe once called the Spice Islands near Asia?

22. What are the two largest islands in the Philippines?

23. What European explorer discovered the Philippines and claimed them for King Philip of Spain?

#23 Web Page Brush-Up

Let's take up another subject for a while: Web page programming. We will do some HTML review. Remember that HTML stands for HyperText Markup Language. It is the language for programming Web pages.

Open up a new file in Wordpad or Notepad. (To find these on a PC, go to Start, then Programs, then Accessories, then find Wordpad or Notepad. Wordpad adds more formatting than Notepad does, and on my computer is easier to save as HTML.) (For help doing this on a Mac, see our Website FAQ.)

Save the empty file as an HTML file. Here's how: click on **Save As**, then on the upper part of the dialogue box choose a place to put it, and on the bottom part of the box choose a format. There isn't any HTML format to choose, so we will choose **Text Document** in Wordpad, or **All Files** in Notepad. On the line for the file name, type in the name plus ".html," like this: Myfile.html. Click on **Save**. You may get a caution message wondering if you really want to get rid of formatting. Click OK.

Now we need to make sure this file has saved as an HTML file. Shrink down the things on your desktop and find your My Computer icon. Click on it, and keep clicking on folders till you find the spot where you stored Myfile.html. Does it have an icon that matches your browser (an e for Internet Explorer, for instance)? If so, it is HTML. If not, double-check by going to the view menu at the top of the folder window and clicking on details. Now you can view the details, and it should tell you the full name of your file. If it appears to be a text file, you need to try to save it again, choosing a different format (**All Files** or **Text Document**, typing .html at the end), until it saves as an HTML file.

OK, now you have a blank HTML file. Let's type some words into it using Wordpad or Notepad.

I hope you remember from *Computer Science Pure and Simple Book 1* that HTML files are formatted using pairs of tags, which are enclosed in angle brackets <like this>. The computer reads what's in the tags and prints out on the page the words that are surrounded by tags. Tags come in nested pairs. The first one of the pair (the on-switch) has no slash; the second (the off-switch) has a beginning slash </like this>.The opening one for your Web page looks like this: <html>, and the closing one for the very end like this: </html>. Just to confuse things, some types of tags don't come in pairs. For example, <br> means line break, or new paragraph, and it doesn't come with a </br> at the end of the paragraph.

Type this into your file:

    <html>
    </html>

Everything we add will be between these two tags, which are telling the computer that this will be an HTML file.

Inside the HTML tags will be two sections: head and body, each with opening and closing tags. The head is for the stuff that goes in the blue band at the top of the Web page. The body is for the stuff that goes on the Web page. Let's add tags and leave space for the words we will be putting in. I will underline what I have just added:

```
<html>
<head>

</head>
<body>

</body>
</html>
```

Notice that these are nested; the pairs go between the opening and closing slash marks. Now, we want to put a title in the **head**. That's the blue band at the top of the finished Web page. Let's add the title, shown below underlined.

```
<html>
<head>
<title> The Frog Story </title>
</head>
<body>

</body>
</html>
```

We want to put in a background color. Add this to the starting body tag:

```
<html>
<head>
<title> The Frog Story </title>
</head>
<body bgcolor="#ff0000">
</body>
</html>
```

It's time to see what this looks like on our Web page. Save it under the same file name (using **Save**, not **Save As**), and then shrink the Wordpad. Using the My Computer icon, find the folder where you put the file, and then click on it. Your browser should pop up showing your file. If it doesn't show, you have made a tiny error in typing. Make sure your code matches mine exactly. You should have a red page with its title in the blue band at the top. Looks a little plain, doesn't it? Let's work on it some more. Shrink the browser (don't close it).

Well, our Web page ought to say something, don't you think? It's a tradition among computer folks (also known as programmers) to type a program that says "Hello, World," in any new computer language they are learning. I suppose this is what a baby would say if it could, when it is born. So let's say, "Hello, World." We have to put it in the body, of course.

```
<html>
<head>
<title> The Frog Story </title>
</head>
<body bgcolor="#ff0000">
Hello World
</body>
</html>
```

Now save the file (you could hit **control-s**). Enlarge your browser. Hmm, it doesn't say Hello World. Do you know why? We haven't refreshed what it is looking at! It is still looking at the old stuff! To refresh it, there may be a refresh icon at the top of the page. It will have two arrows going in circles on it. Pause your mouse over several icons to see if they say "refresh." If not, go to the view menu, and click on **Refresh**. Now the latest is showing! It should say "Hello World." But—it's kind of small!

Should we make that a big headline? How about size h1, the biggest? We need to put h1 tags around our text. Change your code this way:

```
<html>
<head>
<title> The Frog Story </title>
</head>
<body bgcolor="#ff0000">
<h1>Hello World</h1>
</body>
</html>
```

Want to add another line in smaller type, say h2? (We can go all the way down to h6.) Can you guess how? Try it and then look at mine:

```
<html>
<head>
<title> The Frog Story </title>
</head>
<body bgcolor="#ff0000">
<h1>Hello World</h1>
<h2>The Frog Story</h2>
</body>
</html>
```

Now, save your Wordpad file, shrink it, and refresh the browser window. What do you think?

Let's add a picture and create a folder for our Web page. Find a digital image you can use on your computer, a file that ends with .gif or .jpeg. You may have a photo on your computer you can use.

Here's how to find images on a PC. Right click on the **Start** button at the bottom left of the PC screen. Choose the **Search** option. You'll see a screen that looks like this:

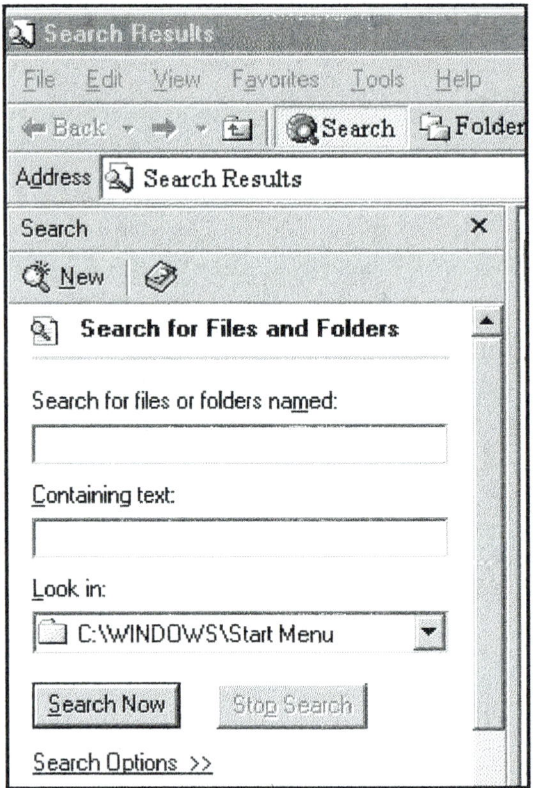

In the top blank, **Search for Files and Folders**, put

    ***.jpeg**

The asterisk, *, means "anything" in DOS, the old system for talking to computers. In the bottom one, **Look In**, click the down arrow and choose "local hard drives (C:)".

Then click on **Search Now**. Click on the files or folders that show up and see what you have. You can also look for ***.gif**, another image format that is Web-compatible.

Assume you found an image. What you really want to know is where it is on the computer. So go to the **Up Folder** icon and click on it, taking note of where you are in the folders.

Now, you need to create a folder to hold your new Web page, and in it you will put the image file you chose, and also the HTML file. To create the folder, click on your My Computer icon and then click on the local hard disk, C. Once that window is opened, go to **File**, then **New**, and **New Folder**. Now type to rename your new folder "BrushUp Webpage."

Next save your HTML file there. Since your Wordpad is shrunk, enlarge it and use **Save As** to save it to the new folder. Don't forget the .html ending!

Next I'll put an image in my new folder. I'll click on the My Computer icon and find the folder with image that I had located using the search a minute ago. I will click again on the My Computer folder and click on folders until I get to the BrushUp Webpage folder. So I have two windows open. I will make the windows smaller by clicking on the small-window icon, in the upper right of the window next to the x—it looks like two boxes. Then I will resize the window by tugging on the lower right corner. Now I will drag and drop files from one folder to another, or use **Copy** and **Paste**, **control-c**, and **control-v**. In the new folder, let's rename the image something nice and short, like pic.gif. To rename, select the name and click the right-hand mouse button, and then go down to rename. Type in the new name. Be sure you still have the .jpeg or .gif ending (don't worry if you can't see it; hopefully it is still there). I will assume its name is now pic.gif.

Now, enlarge your HTML file again and in your code call your image source, or **img src**. Let's put it above the "Hello World."

```
<html>
<head>
<title> The Frog Story </title>
</head>
<body bgcolor="#ff0000">
<img src="pic.gif">
<h1>Hello World</h1>
<h2>The Frog Story</h2>
</body>
</html>
```

Save and take a look using the browser with refresh. Does it look good? Hmm, not really. It needs centering. Let's center it:

```
<html>
<head>
<title> The Frog Story </title>
</head>
<body bgcolor="#ff0000">
<center><img src="pic.gif"></center>
<h1>Hello World</h1>
<h2>The Frog Story</h2>
</body>
</html>
```

Actually, let's center our words too:

```
<html>
<head>
<title> The Frog Story </title>
</head>
```

```
<body bgcolor="#ff0000">
<center><img src="pic.gif">
<h1>Hello World</h1>
<h2>The Frog Story</h2></center>
</body>
</html>
```

Want to play with the size and shape of the picture? Let's put in a size in pixels for the image and see what it looks like. If it looks funny, change the numbers:

```
<html>
<head>
<title> The Frog Story </title>
</head>
<body bgcolor="#ff0000">
<center><img src="pic.gif" width=300 height=200>
<h1>Hello World</h1>
<h2>The Frog Story</h2></center>
</body>
</html>
```

Let's add a link to another Web page. Shrink your HTML file. Now, use Google to find a Web site on frogs, or whatever your topic is. Click on the URL bar and hit **control-c**, to copy the URL to the internal clipboard. Now enlarge your HTML file again. Inside the body (just after the second line that says The Frog Story), type this, changing it to fit what you have:

<a href="http://www.whatevertheWebsite.com"> Check out this site on frogs!</a>

The second part is what shows on your page. The first part is the address where the clicker is sent. Be sure the link has the **http://www** part in it. Notice that for a link, the opening tag contains an **a**, and the closing contains **/a**.

OK, save it. Now we have a brush-up Web page!

Look at it with your browser, clicking on the Refresh icon. Does your link work?

Exercises

1. Change the background color. Experiment with different letter and number combinations and see what you get. Uppercase and lowercase don't matter. For starters, blue is #0000FF, aqua is #00FFFF, yellow is #FFFF00, lime green is #00FF00, silver is #C0C0C0, violet is #AABADD, and light pink is #FDEDF2.

2. Add another image, with a headline below it.

#24 Web Page I

We are going to make another Web site now. Here are the requirements:

- Middle schoolers will make a two-page Web site.

- High-schoolers will make a four-page Web site.

- The home page will be called index.html. Other pages could be called My Hobbies, My Family, etc. (hobbies.html, family.html)

- Each page needs to have the SAME set of links on it linking itself to other pages in the Web site and to itself. To begin, we will make a template page and then copy it a number of times, renaming it each time.

- Each page must have its own paragraph of at least five sentences, a headline, and its own photo or illustration. Absolutely no spelling errors are allowed.

- All these files will be contained in only one folder. This allows you to use one image (a "logo") on all your pages.

- At the bottom of your index page, put at least two links to relevant outside Web pages.

If you have a topic you love, use it! Otherwise we will assume the site provides information about yourself, such as your hobbies, your beliefs, and so on. I'd like you to refrain from using your full real name, since you are a child. Just use your first name. Also, don't put a photo of yourself on the Web. Instead, use photos of what interests you.

Write the headlines and five-sentence paragraphs for each of the pages for your site. You can write them in Word or another word processor. Check the spelling. Gather illustrations to go with them and have them scanned at low resolution, about 70 dpi or dots per inch. You need to have files for these that end in .gif or .jpeg. A picture from a digital camera will work well too; if you have a way to reduce the resolution to 70 dpi, do it. Your tool for doing this might be a photo application such as Microsoft Picture It. Otherwise, a high-resolution image will slow down the loading of your Web page, but you can use it anyway.

#25 Web Page II

We will use a shortcut, Mozilla Composer, to put together our HTML files. We will arrange words and pictures on the screen, and behind the scenes Composer will be putting together an HTML file to match. When we save, it saves as an HTML file that looks like what we have been constructing using Notepad. In fact, we can open it later with Notepad or Wordpad and make changes!

Mozilla is a browser like Internet Explorer. It's an open source project (started by Netscape) which programmers from many companies and many countries work on without pay, in order to provide an alternative to Microsoft. The product is available for free download on the Internet. It has a nifty feature that most other browsers do not: Composer, which you can use to compose Web pages. You can also buy more advanced programs that do this, such as Microsoft Front Page or DreamWeaver. But since Mozilla is free, we will use that for now.

You need a free download of Mozilla from the Internet to your computer. Always download with supervision from an adult, because you could accidentally download harmful stuff. Now type in www.mozilla.org and choose the menu item that will lead you to download the Mozilla browser for your operating system. (Note: Mozilla also has a newer Firefox browser, but that doesn't have Composer in it. Eventually a new version of Mozilla Composer will come out as a separate program, Composer++. Download that if you see it!) Click the download button and download the zipped-up file (remember its name) to your c:\temp folder or your desktop. When the download is done, close the open applications on your computer and, using the My Computer icon, locate the new file and click on it. It will ask to install it, and just keep clicking on "next" until the job is done. Now you have a new icon on your desktop, a snarling dinosaur head.

Click on the icon to open the browser. A question pops up: do you want to make this your default browser? If you click **yes**, this will open instead of Internet Explorer when you get onto the Internet. Best to click **no** for now. You can use Mozilla as a substitute for Internet Explorer if you like, by clicking on the Mozilla icon any time. (Note: You might want to download Firefox too. It is said to be a great alternative to Internet Explorer, and not yet subject to spyware hackers.)

Near the very top center of the Mozilla browser is a menu item called **Window**. Click on that, and move down to choose **Composer**. Another window with a white screen pops up. This is the Composer application, where we can type words and insert images to arrange things the way we want them to look. But meanwhile, in the background, Composer is putting together a matching HTML file. This type of application is called a "What You See Is What You Get" editor or "WYSIWYG"editor. (I am not kidding. It's pronounced *WIZ-zee-wig* according to www.Webopedia.com. Don't you feel sorry for the people learning this stuff who don't speak English?) Not only can we type words and insert images, but we can also run a spell-checker and make links. When we are done, we use **File Save** to put the invisible HTML file in the folder for the Web page.

We will put all the files for our Web site in one folder. For starters, let's make the folder. Find your My Computer icon and click on it. Click on the C: hard drive. Now click on **File New**, then **Folder**. A new folder pops up, ready to have its name changed. Give it your name, like this: Susie Web Page. Inside this folder we will put these files: index.html, hobbies.html, pic1.jpeg, pic2.jpeg, and so on.

Each of our pages will contain links to the other pages and to itself in a band across the top of the page. In this respect, all the pages will be alike. How do we create that? We will make a template, a simple file containing just the links for our Web site pages on it. Then we will copy the template as many times as we have pages on the Web site. We will tailor each copy to make it a different page for real. If you're in middle school, make two pages. If you're in high school, make four.

First let's give our empty template a name. Click **Save As**. A pop-up may ask you for a title; this is what goes in the blue band at the very top of the Web page. You can say your Web site title for that, such as "Susie's Web Page Home." Now save it in the folder you made. We'll call it index.html. It will be our home page eventually.

We'll make a table to hold our links. On many Web sites, this table of links goes down the left side of the page. Unfortunately, Composer won't do that! It will only make tables that fill up the page horizontally; you can't put anything next to them. Oh well! We'll make a band of links that goes across the top of each page.

Here's how. Find the Table icon near the upper right. It looks like a waffle. Click on it. The dialogue box asks us how many columns and how many rows. Do you remember which is column and which is row, in a table? Here's how I remember: a column holds up a porch. It's vertical. So the column is the vertical stack of boxes in the table.

For middle school: let's make two columns and one row, to provide a horizontal band containing two spots for links. Now the question is, what percent of the page width do we want our table to make up? If it's 100 percent, our two links will each be very long. It would be best to make it 50 percent of the page width.

For high school: let's make four columns and one row. Let's make it 100 percent of the page width, or possibly a bit less—maybe 70 percent.

You may want to make the border 0 pixels wide, to make the table look invisible on the finished page. (It will be defined by dotted lines on the Composer screen.) Then click OK.

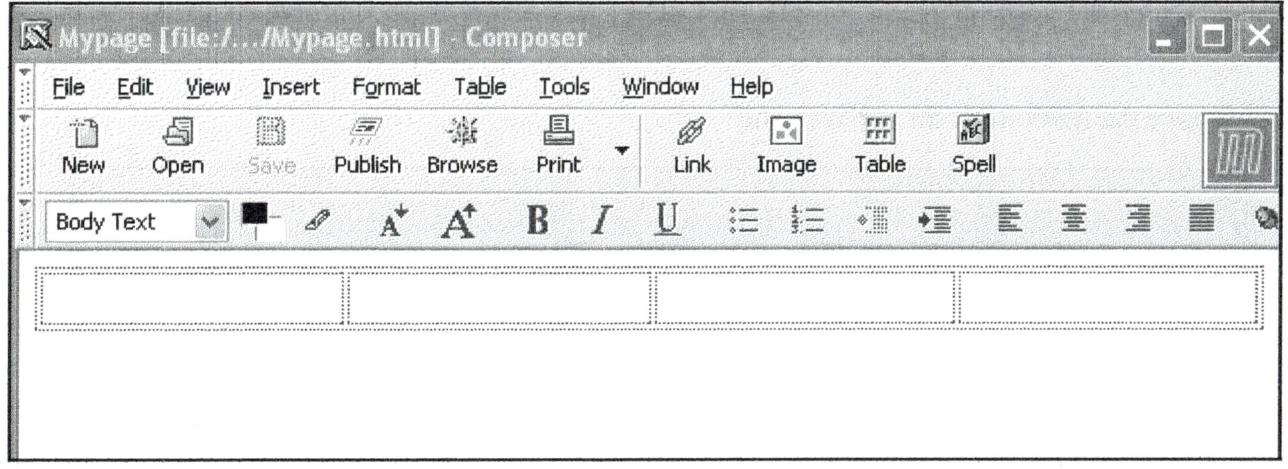

Presto, there's a place to put our links! In the left-hand box, type "Home." That's English for index.html. Now type English names for the rest of your pages in the other boxes, such as Hobbies, Sports, Favorite People, Hobbits, or whatever. Highlight all the link names at once, and align them in the center. You do this by pausing over the icons near the top of Composer until you get to one that says "Align Center."

Let's make these link names into real links. Carefully highlight only the word "Home." Then click on the link icon—it looks like a chain link. There's a place for you to put your URL. (Remember, that's the Web address.) Type **index.html**. Click OK. Now you have a link! Try clicking on it. Oops, it doesn't work! It's not supposed to. Composer is merely grinding out the HTML behind the scenes. You can save the file and open it in a browser, such as Internet Explorer or Mozilla Navigator. Then it would work if the links were all set. But of course they're not yet.

Let me note that a short link like **index.html** is a relative link. It works as long as all the pages you are linking to are in your Web page folder. For ones outside that folder (somewhere else on the Internet) you will need a full URL, starting with http://www.

Now highlight the next link name, say "Hobbies," and type in a file name for it, such as **hobbies.html**. Click OK, and do the same for any remaining links.

Our template is nearly finished. Is there an image you'd like to have at the top of all your Web pages? A logo of sorts, or something you drew? If so, let's put it on this template. Shrink your Mozilla Composer application. Make sure the image you want is a .gif or .jpeg image stored on your computer somewhere. Using your My Computer icon, open a window for your Web site folder. Do the same thing again and open another folder for the spot containing the image file. Copy and paste the image file into the Web site folder.

Now, enlarge your Mozilla Composer application. Put your cursor where you want the picture to go. Click on the Image icon (a white box with shapes in it), near the waffle icon. Browse to locate your picture, and then open it. You can change how it will look by looking through the tabs in the Images popup window. The Appearance tab will let you decide whether to allow text to align in one line alongside it at the top, middle, or bottom, or wrap to the left or right—like a picture in a newspaper. You can also put space around the image, and a solid border. Then click OK to insert it. You can move it around and resize it. When the links and icon look like you want them to, you have a template!

Save the template. This puts a copy in **index.html**. Now use **Save As**, to create more copies. Rename the file to match the link you made: hobbies.html. If you have more links, do **Save As** again and again, using the link names (sports.html, and so on.)

Now we have the framework for our Web site.

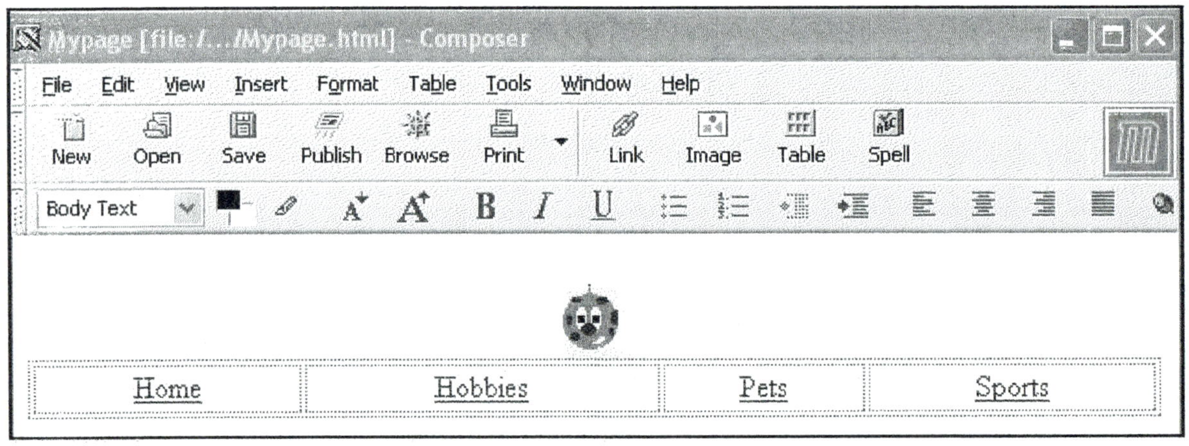

A template

#26 Web Page III

We have a skeleton Web site; now we need to put in some details.

Let's work on the Home page first. It needs a headline that says "Home." In Mozilla Composer, open **index.html**. Beneath the set of links, type the page name. Highlight the name and find the Style box at the top; it should say "normal" or "body text" and has a down-arrow next to the word. Click the down arrow and select H1, the biggest headline size. Align it in the center if it isn't already.

Now we need to add your five sentences of information for the home page. If you have already typed them in Word or Wordpad, open up Word or Wordpad, highlight the text, and copy it to the clipboard by hitting **control-c.** Then enlarge Composer again and paste the text in (**Edit Paste** or **control-v**). Run the spell checker from the Spell icon.

Want to have a colored background for the page? Here's a clue: use the **Help** menu to figure out how. Find the **Help** index, click the **Search** tab on the left, and type in the word "background." Do you figure out how to change the background color? Hint: check out the **Format** menu.

At the bottom of our index page, we want to have at least two links to Web pages we like. So let's go out on the Web and find some. Open a browser and type in www.google.com. Google, the search engine, pops up. Let's type in some keywords for your favorite subject: how about basketball? Read the Google listings to find one that might suit your interests, and click on it. If it has inappropriate content, hit the back button fast! But it probably won't if you read the listings and choose carefully. Find one you really like, and highlight the URL (the address in the band near the top). Copy it using **control-c.** Now, enlarge your Composer and at the bottom of your page, paste the URL using **control-v.** Wait, it's not a link yet! Let's make it one. Highlight it and click on the Links icon. Paste the URL into the links box too. Make sure it contains the first part, **http://.** Click OK. Now it's a link! In fact you can change the wording for what shows on the bottom of the Web page to something in English, like "Michael Jordan," or whatever. Just highlight the words you want to change and start typing the new name. Do this for at least two links. Just above them, put this text: Interesting Links. Be sure to highlight all these and then center them.

Something else for the bottom of your index page: "copyright 2006 by Susie Moore." That's for an official page really going onto the Web. You'll need the name of an adult or your business to put there, instead of Susie Moore. And finally, "Last updated March 3, 2006," using the real date. You'll change that every time you update.

Pictures

Pictures we put on our Web site must be digital, and we must have permission from their creators to use them. We've discussed copyright before, but it doesn't hurt to discuss it again. Let's say you create something—a drawing, a photograph, a poem. You like it and want to keep it. You might put this on it: copyright My Name Current Year. For example, copyright Susie Moore 2004. Now it is legally protected. Anyone who wants to copy it must ask you for permission, even just to photocopy it. If they don't, you can take them to court and require them to pay you lots of money. This is under the law of the United States.

So consider the rights of all those image creators out there. Here are two things you can't do: photocopy images from the library, or paste in images from the Web. In nearly all cases it wouldn't be legal, and it wouldn't be respecting the rights of others. Not only that, but if you put your site on the Internet containing content owned by someone else, the copyright owner might find you and sue you!

Now, there are exceptions to this situation. If the copyright owner declares the image to be "free," we can use the image. There are some of these images on the Internet. For example, regular people go on vacation to New Zealand and are proud of their vacation pictures, so they put them on the Web for anyone to use. Also, some artists are generous in this way too. And there's another way too—you can trace the picture, making a drawing out of it. Now it is no doubt your intellectual property! Just scan it in and create a .jpeg out of it.

We are going to look around on the Internet for some free images to paste in. Shrink down Composer. Get on the Internet and find www.google.com. There is a menu button above the search bar for images. Click on it. Now, in the search bar you get, type in your subject of interest, plus "free," plus ".jpeg." For example, "Gollum free .jpeg."

Read the Google listings carefully before choosing one to open. You are looking for sites with free images of Gollum, or whatever. Careful reading first helps you avoid inappropriate content.

When you open a site and find a picture or animation you like, carefully read all the fine print and make sure the owner has declared to it to be completely free—not just free for desktop wallpaper on one computer. You might want to ask an adult to check it to be sure. If it is free, click on it with the right-hand mouse button, and use **Save As** from that menu. Put it in the Temp folder on your hard drive, or some other folder—not in your Web site folder. Now, enlarge Composer. Click on the image icon. Follow the prompts to insert the image you stored in Temp. (Composer will put it in your Web site folder when you save.)

Our class had difficulty with this lesson in that the pasted images kept vanishing. This was caused by accidentally highlighting the inserted picture, and then hitting any key on the keyboard. If this happens to you, find the **Undo** command under the **Edit** menu and try to undo it. Or you may have to re-paste it. In any case, hit **control-s** to save every few keystrokes. That will save you some time.

What if you have found an image, most likely a photo, which is "free," but the copyright owner wants a link and some credit? Then go back to the Web site and use **copy** to copy the URL, then paste it into your Web page beneath the picture, along with some words like this: *Photo by Mike Smith, used with permission. See http://www.MikeSmith.com.* Paste in the URL, and then highlight it and turn it into a link by pasting the URL into the link box. If you need to ask permission to use what you want, go ahead and email or write the individual to ask permission, and be sure you keep the reply on file in case you are challenged later.

Let's recap what we can use for images:

- We can use images that we create, such as photos or drawings. We can scan our own photos or drawings, creating .gif or .jpeg files that the browsers can use. We can probably also trace a photo, creating a drawing of our own, and scan that.

- We can use digital photos that we take ourselves. We should try to bring the resolution down to 70 dpi (dots per inch) if possible.

- And we can locate pictures on the Web which the creators have decided to let others use "free," not just for desktop wallpaper, but completely free.

- Save the images on your hard drive somewhere. In Composer, put your mouse arrow where you want the picture to be. Using the Image icon (white square with shapes in it), insert your picture. Be sure to save your work, now and often! You don't want a crash or power outage to throw you off.

Now, open another of your pages and add the same stuff: title, paragraph, picture. Then save. Do the same for all of them.

Now it's time to look at your Web page in a browser. You can easily switch over to your Mozilla browser, or you can open Internet Explorer. Using **File Open**, find your **index.html** file. Does it look like what you wanted? If not, open the Composer window and adjust it, then save, and expand the browser again, refreshing the file (Refresh or Reload icons commonly have arrows going in circles on them).

Click on the links. Do they work? They should.

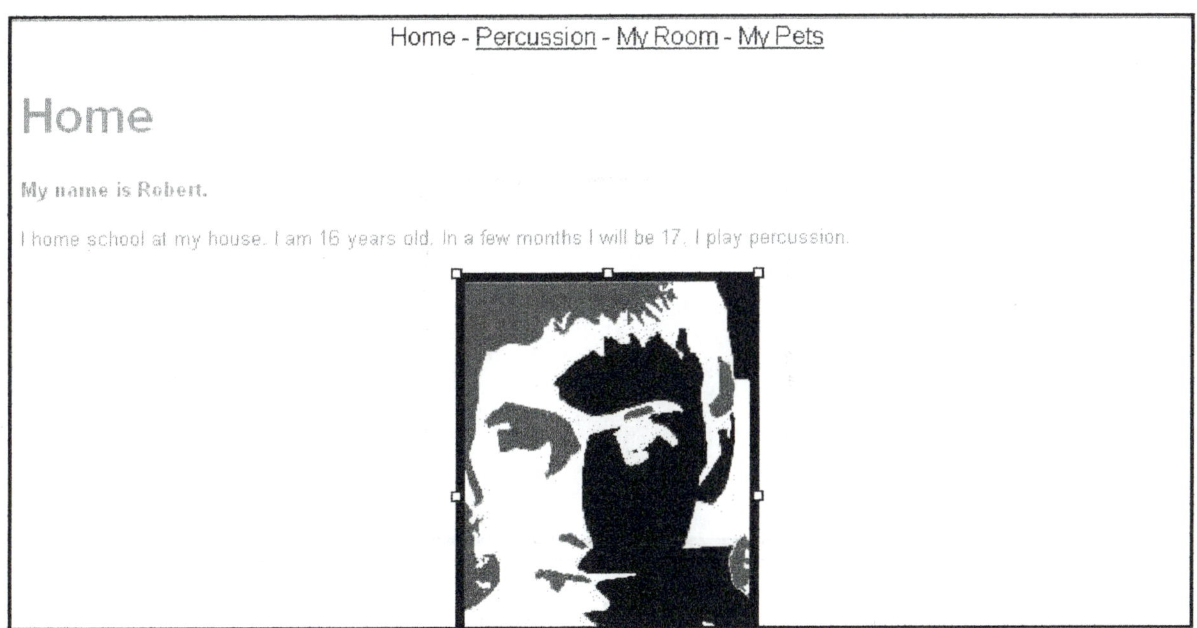

Robert's Home Page

Percussion

i have been taught percussion for almost 8 years.

i like it very much. When I was younger I wanted to be a drummer. But my mom could not find a teacher. So I became a percussionist.

Robert's Percussion Page

My Room

My room is large.

My brothers had my room before me. It has a 10 foot ceiling, and a floor 12 feet by 16 feet. There is a wide space in between my marimba, futon, drum set, desk, and computer. I like to have parties in my room.

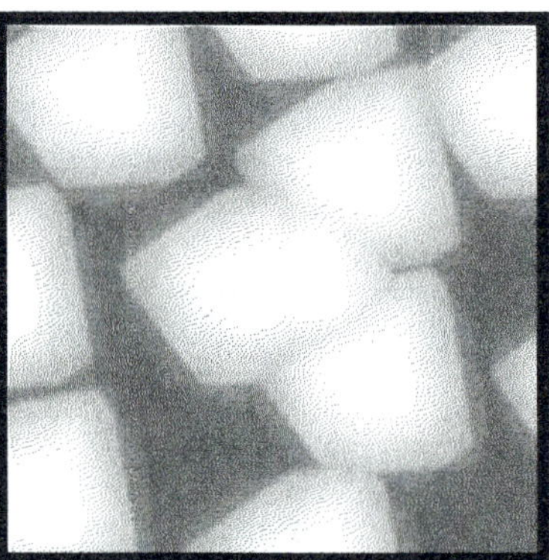

Robert's Room Page

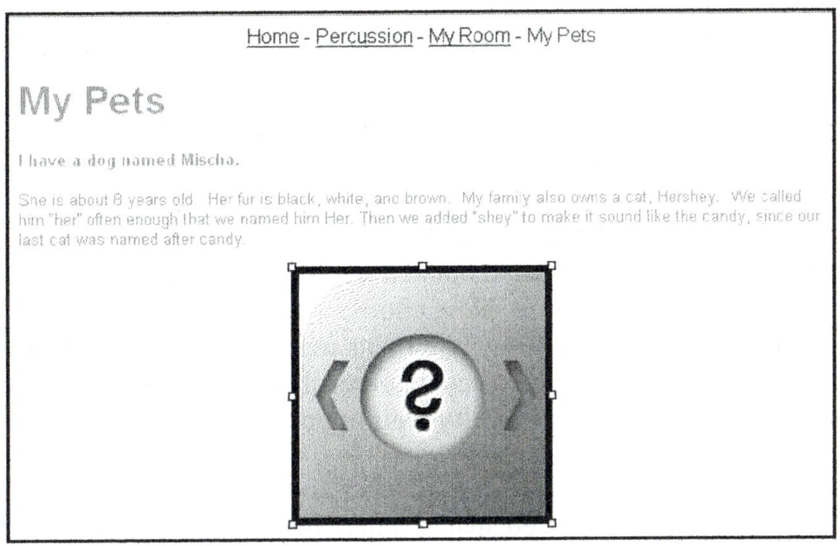

Robert's Pets Page

One more thing. We need to change the title (in the blue band at the top) for each of the new pages. They will all be saying "Susie's Web Page Home" if we don't. What we want is "Susie's Web Page Home" for the index page, and "Susie's Web Page Hobbies" for the hobbies page, and so on. We can make that change by opening the HTML file from the **View** menu, choosing **HTML source**. Edit between the title tags, then save. (We can also do it in Composer from the **Format** menu, **Page Title and Properties**.)

There is a nifty feature that helps us relate the HTML source code to what we are seeing in the WYSIWYG page. At the bottom of the Composer window, there are four tabs: Normal, HTML Tags, HTML Source, and Preview. Experiment with these. The one with HTML Tags is particularly helpful!

Let's check what we've done against our requirements. Did you do them all? Here they are:

- Middle schoolers will make a two-page Web site; High-schoolers will make a four-page site. The home page will be called index.html.

- Each page needs to have the SAME set of links on it linking itself to other pages in the Web site and to itself. To begin, we will make a template page and then copy it a number of times, renaming it each time.

- Each page must have its own paragraph of at least five sentences, a headline, and its own photo or illustration. Absolutely no spelling errors are allowed.

- All these files will be contained in only one folder. This allows you to put one image (a "logo") on all your pages.

- At the bottom of our index page, we will have at least two links to outside Web pages we like.

#27 Putting Your Site on the Web

Now that you have a folder filled with files for your Web page, we need to figure out how to put it on the Web. If you don't want to put it on the Web, go to the end of this lesson now.

First of all, let's arrange the contents in the folder so we can see what we have. Click your My Computer icon and open folders until you have opened the one that contains your Web site. There is a menu item at the top called **View**. Click on it. Now choose **Details**. This arranges your files using words and tiny icons. Now again click on **View**, then **Arrange Icons**, then **By Type**. This will put all your HTML files together and all your image files together. Doesn't that look tidy? Let's try to always look at our Web page file this way. Then it's pretty well organized for us.

First of all, your Internet Service Provider (ISP) may offer some free server space. AOL and AT&T Worldnet both offer members some free Web space; others may as well. If you take them up on this, your Web site will have a URL, or Web address, that says something like www.xyz123.members.aol.com. AT&T Worldnet's space would be www.xyz123.att.net, or something like that. You don't get a recognizeable domain name unless you pay for it.

So, what is a domain? It's the unique identifier for your Web site. Let's consider my Web site, http://www.motherboardbooks.com. In that URL are some letters common to most Web sites. The unique part is motherboardbooks.com. That is my domain name.

Domain Registration

There is an organization called Internic that is in charge of all the registrations on the Internet. It licenses other companies, directly or indirectly, to sell domain registrations. You buy the right to use a unique name for a year or two years or five years. If you renew before it expires, you can keep your name forever. You can also sell it. You can move your registration to another hosting company if you want. A year of registration might cost $15 or $20.

Domain Hosting

This is space on a Web server, or storage computer. Once you have registered your domain, you need to also buy space to put it on, unless you have an Internet server yourself! Your host will handle file transfers and keep your Web page files. It will also handle email for you, if you set up an email account to go with your domain, such as info@motherboardbooks.com. These email accounts are called POP3 accounts, standing for Post Office Protocol 3, the type of file transfer. Domain hosting has costs associated, but in many cases you can get this service free if you agree to let the host put ad banners on your Web site. To get one without a banner, you pay for "bannerless hosting."

It is simplest to have one company do both your registration and your hosting. You aren't stuck with the same company forever; it is possible to change. Most of these companies also offer Web site templates that allow you to easily create a professional-looking Web site. You just answer questions at setup and pay a fee. Most companies offer services in bundles. You can shop around. One word you need to know is *bandwidth*. It has come to mean the amount of data per second that can be stuffed through a Web inlet. The more bandwidth your Web site requires, the longer it takes to load from the Internet down to someone's browser.

Here are some Web host possibilities for you to check. Most of them offer domain registration as well.

- www.emwd.com (owned by a homeschooling family in Virginia)
- www.lowesthosting.com offers a shopping cart and plenty of bandwidth, but has no site-creation tools. This could be a good one for the sites we have created ourselves.
- www.LinuxWebhost.com
- www.churchquest.com, which specializes in nonprofits and churches, but also hosts Christian businesses.
- www.Directnic.com, which has unbundled pricing.
- www.ValueWeb.com
- www.Godaddy.com
- www.Stargate.com

One more thing you need to know: how to get your files onto the remote server. You need a file transfer protocol, or FTP. If you have Internet Explorer, it's easy. (If you don't have Internet Explorer, you may have to buy or download an FTP application. Try to find one that is "drag and drop," as explained below. Mozilla Composer will do the job under the **Publish** icon, but you do have to type or paste in the file names, instead of dragging and dropping.)

To use Internet Explorer, first set up the domain hosting, complete with username and password. In the URL bar, type this: ftp://username:password@mydomain.com. After a few seconds, a folder will appear with the name of your domain on it. Click it to open it. Now, shrink that down and click the My Computer icon on your computer.

We will "drag and drop" the files into the remote folder. Find the folder on your own computer that contains your Web site. Open it and make the window half-sized, using the upper-right-hand icons on the window—one is a dash, one is an x, and one shows two boxes. Click on the two boxes icon, and the window shrinks. Re-size it by using your mouse to tug on the lower right corner. Now, open your browser window and resize that too. Put them next to each other. Now drag and drop the files one by one from the file on your computer to the one on the Web. When you are done, visit your Web site! Type your URL into the URL bar at the top of the browser. If you have problems, your domain host should be able to help you.

I recommend keeping an exact copy of your Web site on your computer, in that folder we created. When you make changes, first, make them to the files in the folder on your computer. Then transfer any files that have changed to the Web server. Don't forget to change that line at the bottom of the page that gives the date of last update! If you have used a template, you can make changes using Wordpad and the HTML file. Now that you know some HTML, it shouldn't be hard to find the right spot to change.

If You Don't Want to Put Your Site on the Web

After doing all this work, you might want to at least make it the default Web page for anyone using your computer. Open your browser and use **File Open** to open your Web page. In Internet Explorer, there is a menu item at the top called **Tools**. In that list, find **Internet Options**, then click the **General** tab. There is a place at the top to make the current Web page the home page; click **Use Current**. Then click OK. Now, whenever anyone opens Internet Explorer on that computer, they will see your Web page first.

Part III: Various Programming Skills

#28 Using a Spreadsheet for Calculations

A spreadsheet is a handy thing, if you know how to use it. In *Book 1* we discussed how you use one to enter data and make graphs. Now we want to see how to program a spreadsheet to do repetitive calculations for you. We'll learn this secret: spreadsheets are really for people who hate arithmetic!

Let's say you want to keep track of what your customers pay you for mowing their lawns. You'll need the information to pay your income taxes. You could keep a record on a piece of paper, like this:

Customer	# times mowed	Price per lawn	Amount paid
Smith	2	$15	2 x $15 = $30
Jones	3	$20	2 x $20 = $40
Williams	2	$45	2 x $45 = $90
Total			30 + 40 + 90=$160

But if you enter this into a spreadsheet, the computer will do the figuring for you. Also, you can make changes easily. Every time you mow the lawn again, you change the number of times mowed, and the spreadsheet will redo all the calculations for you.

Open your spreadsheet program (Excel or another). We have talked about rows and columns before. Do you remember? The rows go across, and the columns go down (think of the columns holding up a porch). Where they intersect, we have cells. Each cell has a name. For example, the cell that is in column E row 3 will be called E3.

Find B3. Starting there, type in the information in the top row. If the cell isn't wide enough, enlarge it by clicking on the very top row, where it says the letter name of the column. Move the cursor sideways to the edge of the column until you get a double-sided arrow. Then click and hold the button down, moving the edge of the column to where you want it.

	A	B	C	D	E	F
1						
2						
3		Customer	# times mowed	Price per lawn	Amount paid	
4						
5						
6						

Our cells can contain words, numbers, and formulas (equations). Let's fill up the cells below our first three headings with the words and numbers we have. (Leave "amount paid" blank.) Don't type a $ sign; we'll insert that in a minute! You can use the tab key to get from one cell to the next, or the arrow keys, or the mouse.

Now it should look like this:

	A	B	C	D	E
1					
2					
3		Customer	# times mowed	Price per lawn	Amount paid
4		Smith	2	15	
5		Jones	3	20	
6		Williams	2	45	
7					

First, let's make the last two columns into dollar formats. Click on the columns headings D and E to highlight them. Now, if your spreadsheet has a $ icon on the tool bar, click it. Otherwise, go to the **Format** menu, then **Cells,** then **Number Formats**, then pick **Currency** from the list, and select OK. Presto! Now we have dollar formats in the last two columns. Problem is, there is nothing showing in the last column yet!!

Here is what we will do: put an equation in cell E4. Click on the cell to highlight it. Now type =. This tells the computer we are about to enter a formula. Notice that in the formula pane at the top, the equal sign shows up! Whatever we type is always echoed up there. This is particularly useful for formulas, which will soon become invisible except for this formula pane.

X ✓ = =

Book1

	A	B	C	D	E
1					
2					
3		Customer	# times mowed	Price per lawn	Amount paid
4		Smith	2	$ 15.00	=
5		Jones	3	$ 20.00	
6		Williams	2	$ 45.00	
7					

Notice the formula pane at the top of this illustration.

What we want in this formula is 2 x 15, or actually *the contents of C4* times *the contents of D4.* Remember that computer-ese multiplication is * and division is / for these formulas. So we can type **=C4*D4**, and press **Enter**. Presto! the computer uses the formula and calculates a 30 for the answer! (If you get "#Name" in a cell, it means there is something wrong with your formula.) To see our formula, we click on the cell to highlight it, and the formula shows above in the formula pane. Does it look right?

E4	▼	=	=C4*D4	

Book1

	A	B	C	D	E
1					
2					
3		Customer	# times mowed	Price per lawn	Amount paid
4		Smith	2	$ 15.00	$ 30.00
5		Jones	3	$ 20.00	
6		Williams	2	$ 45.00	
7					

Now, let's fill in the next cells down the same way, with =C5*D5 and =C6*D6. Did you get dollar amounts in the cells?

OK, let's clear them now and try something else. Click on E5 and clear it using **Backspace Enter**. Do the same for E6.

Now, let's fill in those cells in a little easier way. We don't actually have to type the cell names. We can just click on the cell to add it to the formula. Here's how. Click on the Amount Paid formula cell for Jones, E5. Type = to show the computer a formula is coming. What we want to add is "=C5*D5". Click the actual cell, C5. Notice that the C5 pops into the formula. Type the * for multiplication. Now click on the actual cell, D5. Hit **Enter**. Presto!

E5	▼	=	=C5*D5	

Book1

	A	B	C	D	E
1					
2					
3		Customer	# times mowed	Price per lawn	Amount paid
4		Smith	2	$ 15.00	$ 30.00
5		Jones	3	$ 20.00	$ 60.00
6		Williams	2	$ 45.00	
7					

And one more way to fill those cells. Let's clear cells E5 and E6 again by clicking on them and pressing **Backspace Enter**. We are going to **Fill Down**. This way is the most useful if we have a long list. A spreadsheet will take a cell or cells in a row and duplicate them going down the sheet as far as you want. In this case we want only two more, so it isn't too dramatic. But this **Fill Down** can save you a lot of typing!!

What we want is to fill down the next formula cells in a fashion nearly the same as the cell above them. So we highlight first the cell that we will copy, the one that currently says $30.00. We hold down the mouse button and also highlight the blank two below it. So all three are highlighted. Now we go to the **Edit** menu and find **Fill,** then **Fill Down**. Numbers pop into the blank cell. Are they the right ones? We are wondering if the formulas are just pasted from the cell above, in which case they would be the wrong formula, referring to the wrong row. So let's look at the formula in E6. We can highlight that cell and look above at the formula pane.

E6		▼		=	=C6*D6	

Book1

	A	B	C	D	E
1					
2					
3		Customer	# times mowed	Price per lawn	Amount paid
4		Smith	2	$ 15.00	$ 30.00
5		Jones	3	$ 20.00	$ 60.00
6		Williams	2	$ 45.00	$ 90.00
7					

Sure enough, it says =C6*D6, which is what we want! The **Fill Down** command is so smart that it changed the cell addresses in the formula!

Let's practice some more with **Fill Down**. Highlight the $45 in the last row, and also highlight down five or six cells below it. Go to **Edit**, then **Fill**, then **Down**. Presto! Each cell says $45 now! It's like using the **Paste** command. So we can use **Fill Down** for cells that contain numbers as well as formulas. Now, clear those cells with the extra $45 in them. Clear them this time by selecting all of them and going to **Edit**, then **Clear Contents.** You can also clear them by pushing the **Delete** button on your keyboard.

Let's make a total for the spreadsheet. We'll highlight all the numbers in the last column, including a blank one below the last number. Find an icon that looks like this: Σ This is the Greek letter sigma, or S for Sum. Click on the Sigma icon, and presto, a total number appears beneath them!

If you can't find the Sigma icon, go to **Insert**, then **Formula**. Choose the formula **Sum**. Fill in the cell addresses if they aren't filled in already, with the cells that you highlighted. You can write E4:E6 as shorthand for E4, E5, E6.

If you get some gobbledygook, select the cell, go to the formula pane, and edit it so it looks like it should, namely

    =Sum(D4:D6)

Here are some error codes you might get in a cell:

- #Ref! means you have misused a cell address.

- #Name? means your formula isn't using proper syntax. To see what the syntax should be, go to **Insert Function** (choose the function) and press **Enter**. Look for a model use of the function showing proper commas and parentheses. *Function* is another word for *procedure*.

- #Num! means your formula has a problem with a numerical value.

Now that we have a total value at the bottom of "Amount paid," let's label that row as "total." Here's
our spreadsheet:

Customer	# times mowed	Price per lawn	Amount paid
Smith	2	$ 15.00	$ 30.00
Jones	3	$ 20.00	$ 60.00
Williams	2	$ 45.00	$ 90.00
Total			$ 150.00

Let's tinker a little. Pretend the summer is going by. Let's add one to the "times mowed" for each
customer. Click on each cell and edit the number, then hit **Enter.** What happens? It automatically
updates everything else, even the total!

Customer	# times mowed	Price per lawn	Amount paid
Smith	3	$ 15.00	$ 45.00
Jones	4	$ 20.00	$ 80.00
Williams	3	$ 45.00	$ 135.00
Total			$ 215.00

Exercise

Make a spreadsheet for this situation:

You are organizing lemonade stands run by your brothers and sisters. You are paying each of them $1
per hour, or $1.50 per hour, depending on their ages. You are keeping track of their hours and need to
pay them. But how much? You decide to use a spreadsheet so you can change the numbers every week
and you don't have to recalculate too.

Make a spreadsheet that says:

Name   Rate of pay   Number of hours worked   Amount owed

Insert this information: your employees Rachel and Robert are paid $1 per hour, and Richard and
Robin are paid $1.50 per hour. Rachel and Robert have worked 2 hours, Richard 3, and Robin 4. How
much do you owe each? What is the total?

Once you have that figured out, increase everyone's rate of pay by $1. Now what do you owe them?

Save your work. You'll need it for the next lesson. Also print it out to show your teacher.

#29 Procedures, or Functions, in a Spreadsheet

Guess what, folks, we have learned all about procedures in MicroWorlds. These procedures, also called functions, are the way that computers think. And spreadsheets use them too! There are built-in functions for calculating average, sum, and so on, and also one called "IF." Sound familiar?

Let's take our spreadsheet about mowing lawns.

	A	B	C	D	E
1					
2					
3		Customer	# times mowed	Price per lawn	Amount paid
4		Smith	2	$ 15.00	$ 30.00
5		Jones	3	$ 20.00	$ 60.00
6		Williams	2	$ 45.00	$ 90.00
7					
8					
9					
10		total			$ 180.00
11					

What if we would like to know the average price we are charging for mowing a lawn? This might seem silly but could be a useful thing to know if we have lots and lots of lawns. You remember that the average of several numbers is simply their sum, divided by the number of them. To get the average of 3, 4, and 5, you add them up, getting 12. You see that were three numbers, and so you divide 12 by 3, and get 4. This is the average of the numbers 3, 4, and 5.

There is a built-in function in your spreadsheet for calculating average. It looks like this: Average( ) Inside the parentheses go the inputs. For this function these are the cell addresses of the numbers you want to average, separated by commas. Like this:

Average(D4, D5, D6)

Other spreadsheets besides Excel may require semicolons instead of commas.

When they are all in the same column like that you can use shorthand, D4:D6. This means D4 through D6. So you want the formula in the cell to look like this:

= Average(D4:D6)

You can click on the cell and type that in, or there is a shortcut. Highlight the cell and then click on the Function icon, if you have one. It looks like this: f_* . This screen pops up:

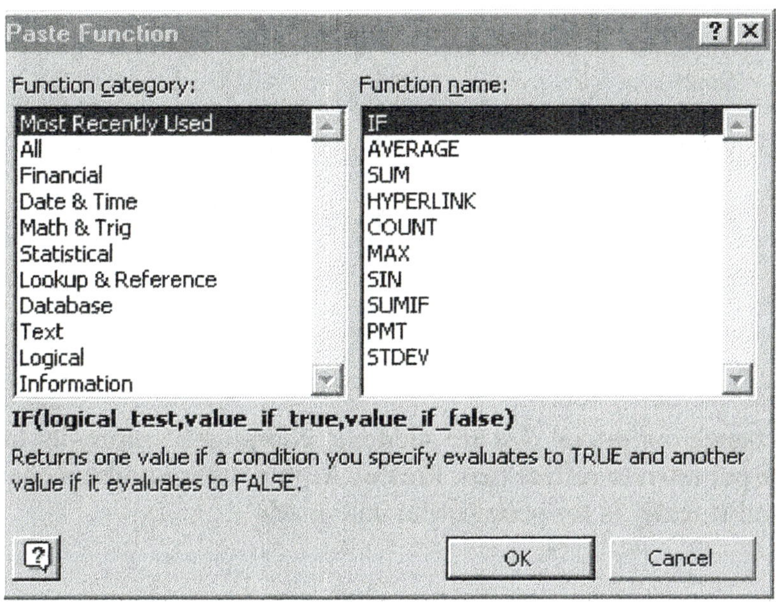

Then choose your function, **Average**, from the list of most-recently-used functions on the right. If it's not there, click on the "all" category on the left, and then find it on right.

Once you choose **Average**, you get another dialogue box that suggests you want to put in D4:D7. Is this right? it asks.

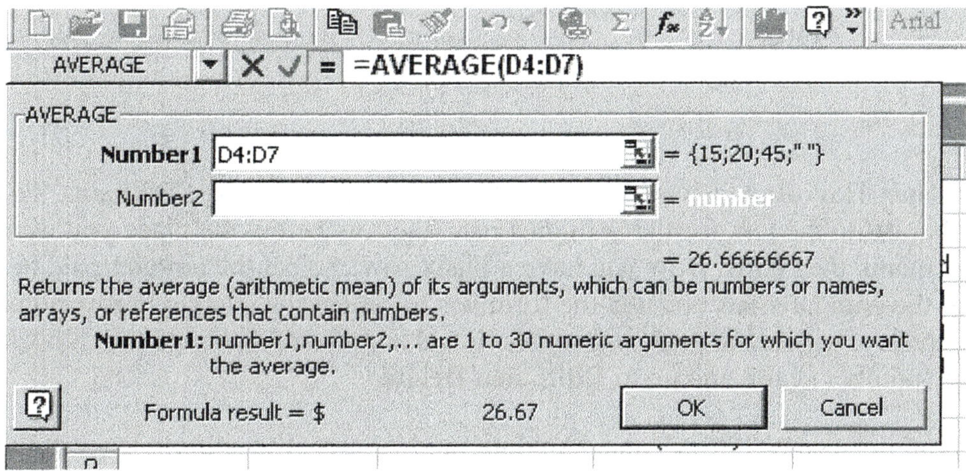

Click OK, and there you are! Or you could edit the D4:D7 to say D4:D6, or C:4, C:5, D:6, or whatever you like, then click OK.

A third way to enter a function is to select the cell, and then go to the **Insert** menu, then **Function**. You get the same dialogue box as above.

So now, highlight the cells D4 to D7, and using each of these methods, create a cell that calculates the average price you are charging for lawns. Let's label that average, so we know what it is, like this:

Customer	# times mowed	Price per lawn	Amount paid
Smith	2	$ 15.00	$ 30.00
Jones	3	$ 20.00	$ 60.00
Williams	2	$ 45.00	$ 90.00
Average		$ 26.67	
total			$ 180.00

Now, let's go in and change our prices. We are suddenly charging $5 more per lawn. Change the three cells that contain price per lawn to reflect that. Presto! All the other numbers change too! This is the beauty of a spreadsheet! It really is for people who hate math!

Customer	# times mowed	Price per lawn	Amount paid
Smith	2	$ 20.00	$ 40.00
Jones	3	$ 25.00	$ 75.00
Williams	2	$ 50.00	$ 100.00
Average		$ 31.67	
total			$ 215.00

Let's add a customer. How about Elvis? Put a line for Presley in just above Williams. To do that, click on the row number off to the left, for the Williams row (the row below the place you want to insert). Go to the **Insert** menu, then **Row**. Now you have a blank row! Select the amount paid to Williams, and you will see that the computer has updated the formulas to reflect the change in row number for Williams. Add Presley, with some data, and see the totals and average change too. Now delete Elvis—highlight the row number again, and go to **Edit**, then **Delete**.

Let's add a column in between "Price" and "Amount paid." Select the column letter at the top for the "Amount paid" column. (The new column will go to the left of the one you select.) Go to **Insert**, then **Column**. Presto, there's the new column! Now, check the formulas to see if they have changed. Select a cell in "Amount paid" and look at the formula pane. Is it different now? It should be. Now, get rid of it—highlight the column letter, and go to **Edit**, then **Delete**.

Now, let's find the function **IF**. Click on the Function icon. First find the right category on the menu on the left. In this case it is a logical function we want. So we click on **Logical**. A list appears on the right. Select **IF**.

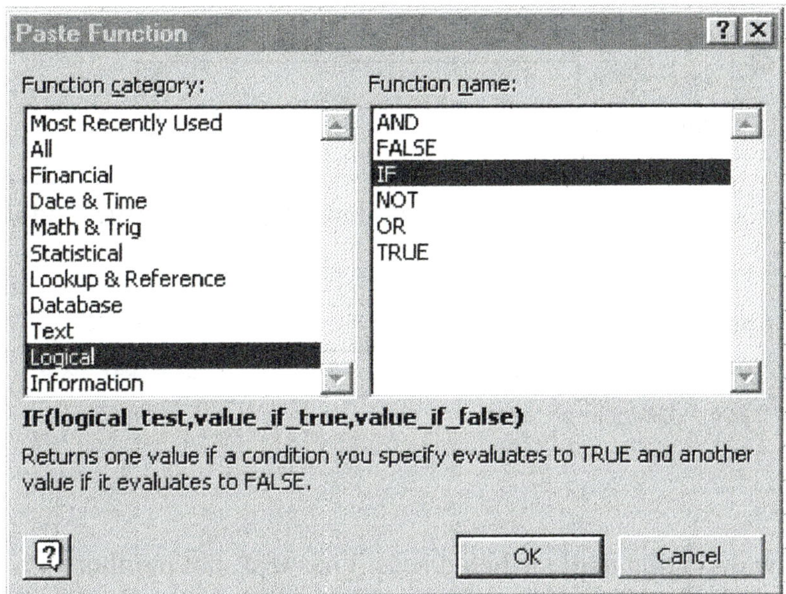

In bold print just below the white boxes we see the format for an **IF** function:

IF(logical_test, value_if_true, value_if_false)

This means that in our formula pane, we need to have this format for this cell. Does this look something like Logo to you? It's no surprise—computer languages, even spreadsheets, have many things in common!

Let's say we want to test to see if our earnings have hit $225. If they have, we need to pay taxes on them! (This is just supposing, of course.) So our test is this: is the total value in E10 greater than 225? If it is, we want to print just beneath it: "pay taxes." Otherwise we will print "pay no taxes."

First we select the cell just below the total. Now using the menu **Insert**, then **Function**, we can choose **Logical**, then **IF**. Click OK. Now we have a dialogue box asking for the inputs for the function—the items in parentheses.

Here is what it currently says:

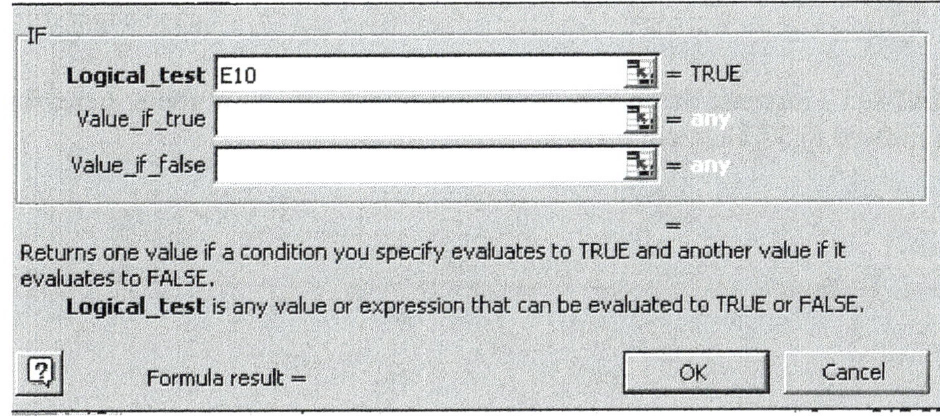

This is silly. E10 is a cell location, not a true-false test. Let's put our true-false test in instead:

139

Let's add our "values," or words that we want printed in E11 if this is true, and if it is false.

The computer adds the quotation marks when it sees it has text, not numbers. Press **Enter**, and we get more quotation marks. Then it inserts the result into the formula pane. We could have typed it in there ourselves, too!

We still have cell E11 selected. Now our spreadsheet looks like this. Note the contents of cell E11 shown in the formula pane at the top.

E11	▼	=	=IF(E10>225,"pay taxes!","pay no taxes!")		

	A	B	C	D	E
1					
2					
3		Customer	# times mowed	Price per lawn	Amount paid
4		Smith	2	$ 20.00	$ 40.00
5		Jones	3	$ 25.00	$ 75.00
6		Williams	2	$ 50.00	$ 100.00
7					
8		Average		$ 31.67	
9					
10		total			$ 215.00
11					pay no taxes!

Well, does it work? Let's increase the income so it goes over $225. How about increasing Smith's number of times mowed to 3? That will do it.

Customer	# times mowed	Price per lawn	Amount paid
Smith	3	$ 20.00	$ 60.00
Jones	3	$ 25.00	$ 75.00
Williams	2	$ 50.00	$ 100.00
Average		$ 31.67	
total			$ 235.00
			pay taxes!

It works!

One last thing about spreadsheets. You can make them look nice. Let's go to the **Format** menu and select **Autoformat**. Choose one of the pre-planned formats, like this:

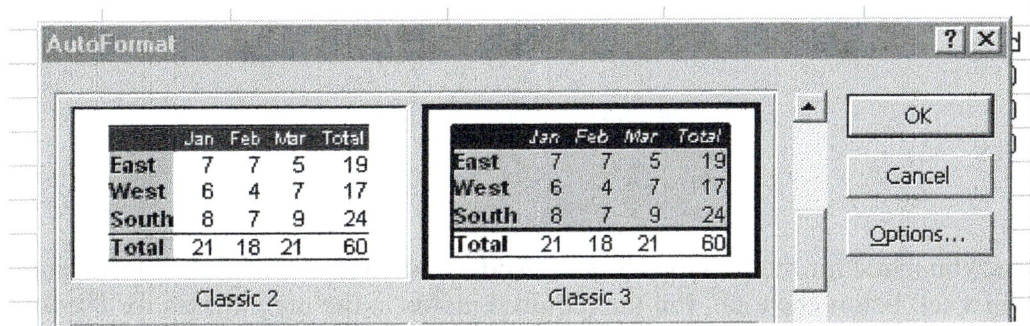

Then click OK.

Oops, my spreadsheet looks funny!

Customer	# times mowed		Price per lawn	Amount paid
Smith	3		$ 20.00	$ 60.00
Jones	3		$ 25.00	$ 75.00
Williams	2		$ 50.00	$ 100.00
Average			$ 31.67	
total				$ 235.00
				pay taxes!

I must have pre-selected just those cells! Let's try it again. I will select all the cells that make up my spreadsheet, with "Customer" at the upper left and "pay taxes!" at the lower right. Now I will go to **Format**, then **Autoformat**, pick one, and click OK.

Customer	# times mowed		Price per lawn	Amount paid
Smith	3		$ 20.00	$ 60.00
Jones	3		$ 25.00	$ 75.00
Williams	2		$ 50.00	$ 100.00
Average			$ 31.67	
total				$ 235.00
				pay taxes!

Ooh, that looks very nice!

Exercise

Open the spreadsheet you made for the previous lesson. Add an average and a total. Choose another function to display in a cell below the total. Put the required inputs in the parentheses for the function. Label the rows for your functions, off to the left.

#30 The Next Step: DOS

We will now take a step backward in time to learn the old way to talk to a computer, DOS. So, why do we want to go backward? We will need it if we continue on our path to become junior programmers. The next language to learn is C, and to use it inexpensively we have to know DOS! That's so we can use the free downloaded C compiler, which works with DOS. The same goes for the language after that, Java.

DOS stands for Disk Operating System. It's the way we used to control computers in the days when there was only a keyboard, no mouse. In addition, what we saw on the screen back then was far simpler and took up a lot less memory space. When the mouse arrived, the new accompanying screens were called Graphical User Interface, or GUI. Perhaps you have seen that acronym before on the T-shirt of some computer person. GUI is everywhere now. It's pretty rare to see the older black style of computer screen. Sometimes you do see it in a store or a medical office, though. You navigate these black screens using the arrow keys, tab keys, and pushing **Enter**.

Guess what? Inside every Windows PC is a DOS PC. So in order to take this journey into history, all we have to do is find the DOS prompt on our PC. It might call itself MS-DOS, for Microsoft DOS. Or it might call itself Command Prompt.

So, let's try to find it. Point to the **Start** button. Point to **Programs**, then **Accessories**, and then click **MS-DOS** or **Command Prompt**. It might look something like one of these:

Here's an idea: let's put a shortcut to the MS-DOS prompt on our desktop. First we have to search for the file. We'll use the Windows Explorer. Go to the **Start** button again, but this time click on it with the RIGHT-hand mouse button. A little dialogue box pops up. One of the possibilities is **Explore**. This is the Windows Explorer, not the Internet Explorer. Click on it.

This is a very handy tool for seeing what is on your computer. On the left, you see all your file folders. A little plus sign next to a folder means that the folder has contents, like this:

    ⊞ 🗀 LHSP

If you click on one, the contents show, and the plus sign becomes a minus sign. If you click on it again, the contents fold up inside the folder once more.

What we are looking for is the **Search** application, to find MS-DOS or Command Prompt. So look up at the top of the window:

You see a **Search** menu item. Click on it. You get a dialogue box. Type in **MS-DOS** or **Command**.

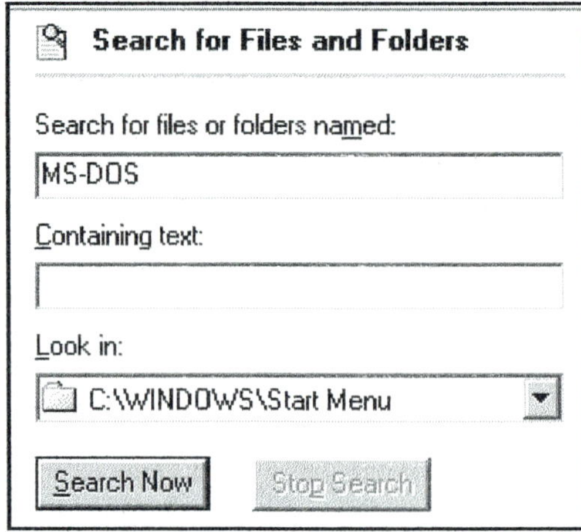

Click **Search Now**.

Now it comes back with a location for the file:

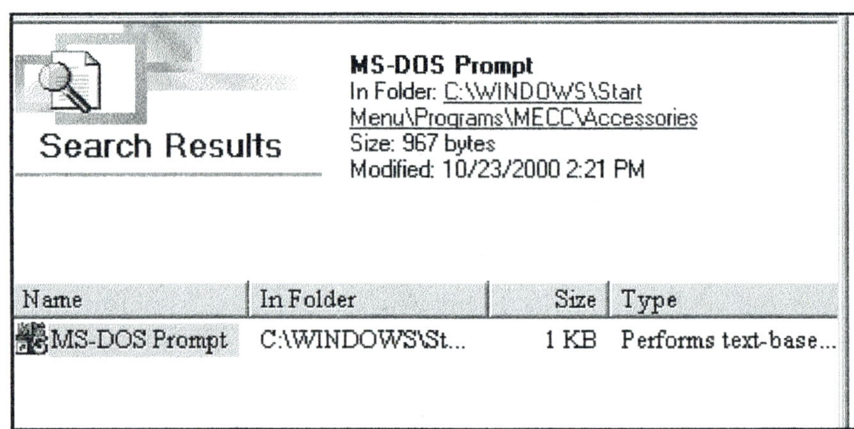

We want to make a shortcut to the file and put it on our desktop. Shortcuts are small pointer files that point to where the file really is. We don't want the file on our desktop because it's too big. The desktop is full of other shortcuts already. So here's how we make one.

Make sure the file is selected, that is it's shaded in. At the top of the window, click on **File**, then **Create Shortcut**. We get an error message:

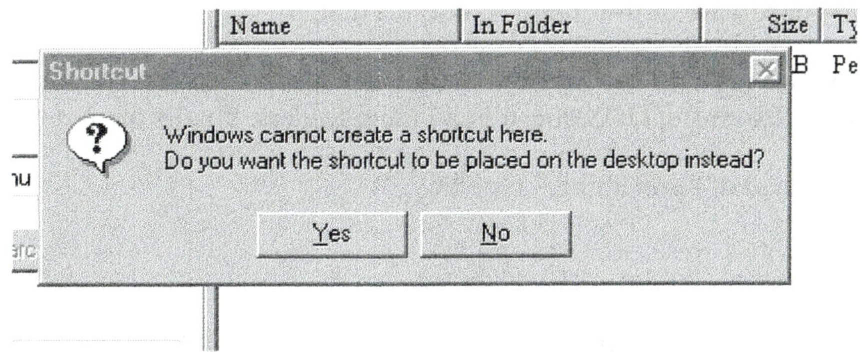

Click Yes. Now we have a shortcut on the desktop where we wanted it! If we had been able to create a shortcut in the other folder, we would have used **Edit**, then **Copy** (control-c), then moved to the desktop and used **Paste** (control-v).

OK, now we have a shortcut on our desktop to the DOS prompt. Let's double click on it.

Now we see a window containing DOS. Here's what mine looks like:

Right after "C:\Windows\Desktop>" is a blinking cursor. If I type something, it goes right there.

So, what are we looking at, anyway?

Let's imagine that we are microscopic people trying to find our way around our computer. We are used to finding our way around using a map. The map tells us where we are; we just have to look at it. (This is like the file system under the My Computer folder, or the Windows Explorer we were just looking at.)

Now suppose we are still little people wandering around in the computer, but now we don't have a map. In fact, we just have a message unit that uses codes. We still have to get around, though. The unit will tell us the name of the place where we are, *if we ask,* using the codes. This is like MS-DOS.

The codes are typed—uppercase or lowercase, it doesn't matter.

There's one big difference right off the bat between the new code and what we are used to. We are used to storing files in *folders*. But DOS doesn't call them folders. It calls them *directories*.

Let's find out more. Instead of "something," type this:

DIR Enter

This means *directory*. Presto, the computer responds with a whole bunch of stuff!

```
ONE-ON~1  LNK               359   10-31-0
REALPL~1  LNK               422   01-22-0
KODAKE~1  LNK               606   12-30-0
REALJU~1  LNK               473   04-14-0
COMMAND   PIF               967   01-24-0
WORDPAD   LNK               441   01-18-0
          25 file(s)            207,662
           2 dir(s)           6,248.78 M

C:\WINDOWS\Desktop>
```

In fact, this is a list of all the shortcuts on your desktop—the contents of the directory you are in. Notice that some of them end in "~1 LNK." The ~1 means that the file name broke a DOS rule, which is that file names have to have no more than eight letters. They can also have a three-letter extension (LNK, or DOC, or HTM, for example). LNK is the extension for a shortcut. DOC is the extension for a Word document. Now that we are using DOS, we will try to name our files with eight letters or fewer, plus a three-letter extension..

So, we are standing in the desktop directory. How do we get out of it? We can't click on a folder, like we did in Windows. Let's try typing **CD**, for change directory.

Hmm, it just tells us what directory we are still in. We need to give it an input to the **CD** command to get it to change to another directory.

Perhaps you remember the dot-dot convention, "**..**", from our Web design in Book 1. This means "go up a level." It can be input for the procedure **CD**, and there should be a space between **CD** and the dots. In this case if we type **CD ..** we will change directory to the directory (folder) that holds the directory that we are in. For instance, if we were in this directory or folder called **MSDRAW** in the picture below, and we typed **CD ..** , we would land upward in the folder that contains **MSDRAW**, namely **MsApps**.

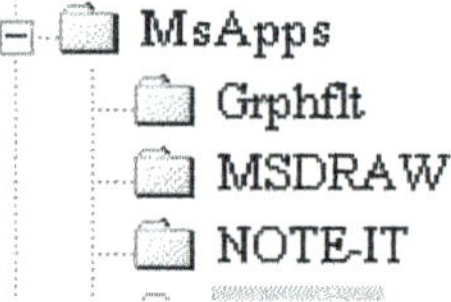

So, let's see what directory we land in if we type "**CD ..**" at our DOS prompt.

```
C:\WINDOWS\Desktop>CD ..

C:\WINDOWS>
```

Presto! We are now in the folder that is up a level, namely **Windows**! Can we go back to where we were? Type **CD Desktop**. Here the input for CD is a file inside the directory we are in, **Desktop**. That puts us down a level—we go back into **Desktop**. Now, type **CD ..** again. We to up a level! Oh, I'm getting a little dizzy. To climb up out of Windows, type **CD ..** again.

```
C:\WINDOWS\Desktop>CD ..

C:\WINDOWS>cd desktop

C:\WINDOWS\Desktop>cd ..

C:\WINDOWS>cd ..

C:\>
```

We are now at the "root" of the C drive. The root is indicated by the **:** . This means there isn't any directory (folder) containing us now except for the C: drive itself, which is physically the hard drive of the computer. Remember, your computer most likely also has an A: drive (for floppy disks) and a D: drive (for CD-ROMs). It may have other drives too.

What are the other files and directories in the root directory? Let's find out by typing **DIR**. This means directory listing. Whew, we see all the files at the root of our C drive! If your computer is like mine, that is a lot. It goes by too fast to read. We don't get as much information as we would using Windows Explorer.

Pick one of these folders (directories) and move into it using a DOS command. Can you figure out how? Now move out again.

*(Answer: Type **CD foldername** Enter   Type **CD ..**)*

Now let's make a new directory. We'll call it **Test**. Remember, it can't have more than eight letters. Here's the code for making a directory: **MD**. So to make **Test**, we'll type **MD Test**.

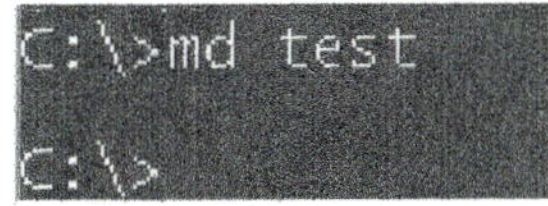
```
C:\>md test

C:\>
```

Hmm, did it do anything? We can't tell, since we can't see a folder pop into existence like in Windows. It's like we're blindfolded! Let's try stepping into the folder/directory. Type **CD Test**, for change directory test.

147

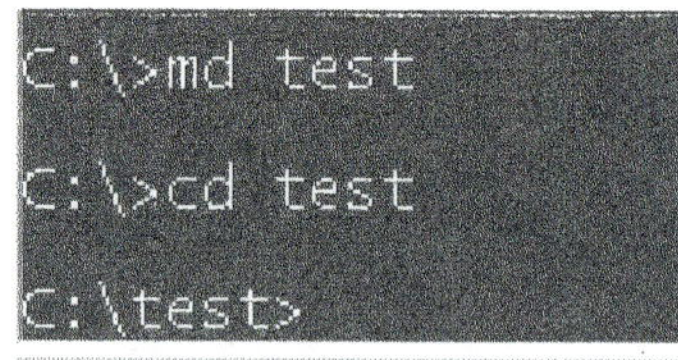

Sure enough, we can go and stand in it, so it's there! Let's shrink down our DOS window and go look for **test** in Windows Explorer. Right click on the **Start** button and click on **Explore**. Then look for a folder called **Test** that is in the root part of the C: drive.

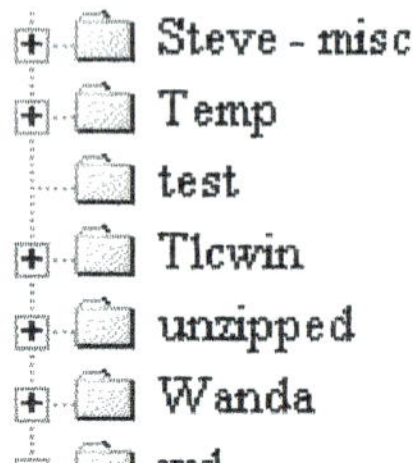

There it is!

Remember that DOS only likes file names with eight letters. Just for grins, let's see what happens when we make a folder with a name that is too long. Go back to the DOS prompt and type in **MD testtesttest**. What happens? What do you know, my post-DOS PC is compensating! It seems to be making a file with a name that is too long! But wait. Let's check to see how it's actually stored. Go up a level to the directory containing the new file (remember how? CD ..). Then ask for a directory listing (DIR). Here's what we get:

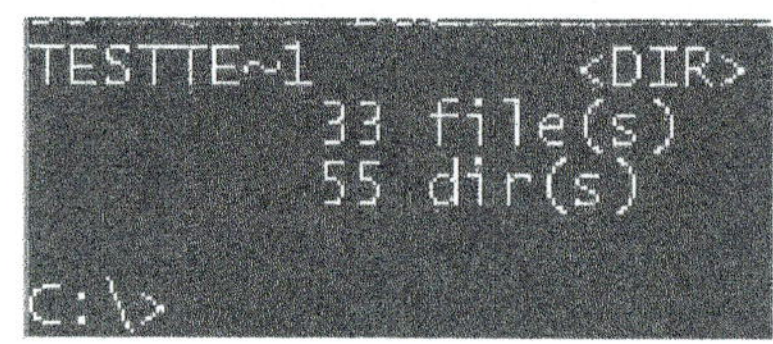

It's **testte~1**. Hmm, it really has only eight letters. The operating system is translating the longer name into the shorter name **testte~1**.

Now, let's get rid of these files. Type **RD test**, for remove directory test, then **RD testtesttest**. Let's check: type **CD test.** Do you get an error message? You should.

Let's go up a level, back to the root of C:. We'll make another folder at the root called **borland**. You'll need one like this to hold your C application download. Can you do it? Change to this directory ("stand" in it).

*(answers: **CD ..**   **MD borland**   **CD borland**)*

Now we're standing in C:\borland. What if we want to go to the place where we started? We need input for **CD** which is a path to get us there. This is a string of codes that tells us where to walk in the folders/directories to get to where we want to go. First we need to go up a level, so we'll start with **..** Then we'll go "down" into the folder **Windows**, and then "down" into the folder **Desktop**:

\windows\desktop

We'll string all that together and use it for our input to **CD:**

CD ..\windows\desktop

```
C:\borlandc>cd ..\windows\desktop

C:\WINDOWS\Desktop>
```

So, when you see the phrase "pathname" on the Internet, this is what they are talking about—a string of codes that tells you how to get blindly from one folder to another, inside a Web site. By the way, the slashes on the Internet pathnames tilt the other way.

Now, how do we get out of DOS?

To get out of the DOS window, we can type **exit** at the DOS prompt. To switch between a full DOS screen and a window, press **alt-enter**. Or, we can use the x in the corner of the window to close the window. Go ahead and close your DOS window.

Download C

The next step in our junior programmer journey is learning the C programming language. After that, you should work on learning Java. But C definitely comes first!

If you are wanting to move on now to a book that teaches C, you could use a free C download from the Internet. I will show you how. We are going to put it in our new file, **borland**.

First, let's open our browser and go to www.google.com. Type in **C free download**. One of the first URLs we see says "C++ Builder downloads," and uses the word "free." The URL for it is this: www.borland.com/bcppbuilder/freecompiler/. Borland is the maker of the C compiler. The maker is obviously the place to get something. So click on this one.

On the page find the compiler. This is what we need for our C study. A compiler is a program that takes code written in the language, in this case C, and compresses it into something else that the computer can rip through really quickly. When we were using MicroWorlds, the compiler was working invisibly. But now we will have to compile our programs before we can run them. So we need a compiler. We could also use a Turbo Debugger to help us debug. Let's download both of these to our **borland** folder.

Click on **compiler**. There is a license agreement to read and agree to. The software is copyrighted, meaning that the creator owns all the rights to it, and is granting you the right to install and use it but not share it with someone else.

Read the agreement, click "I agree" at the bottom (and do what it says, in the future). Here's your download screen:

	Download ftp	Download http
Download size (8.7Mb)	freecommandLinetools.exe	freecommandLinetools.exe

We'll download with http protocol, so click that one. We get a warning screen, which comes every time we want to download:

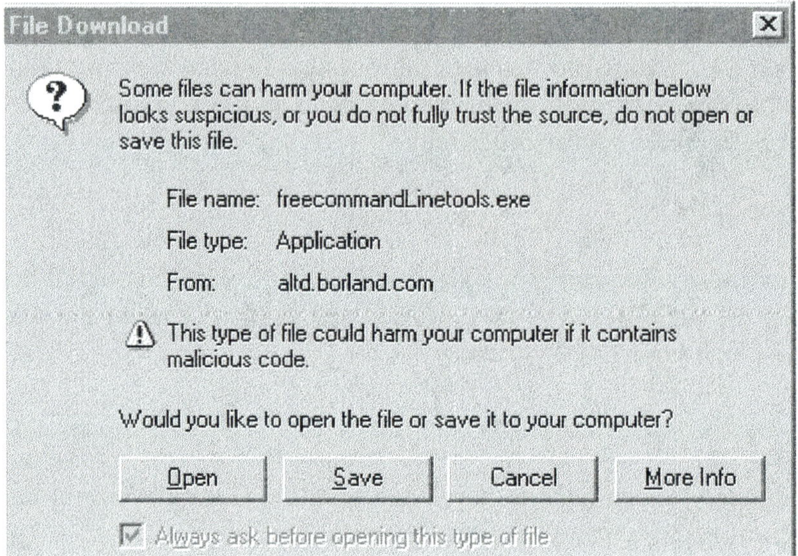

Go ahead and click **Save**.

The computer asks us where.

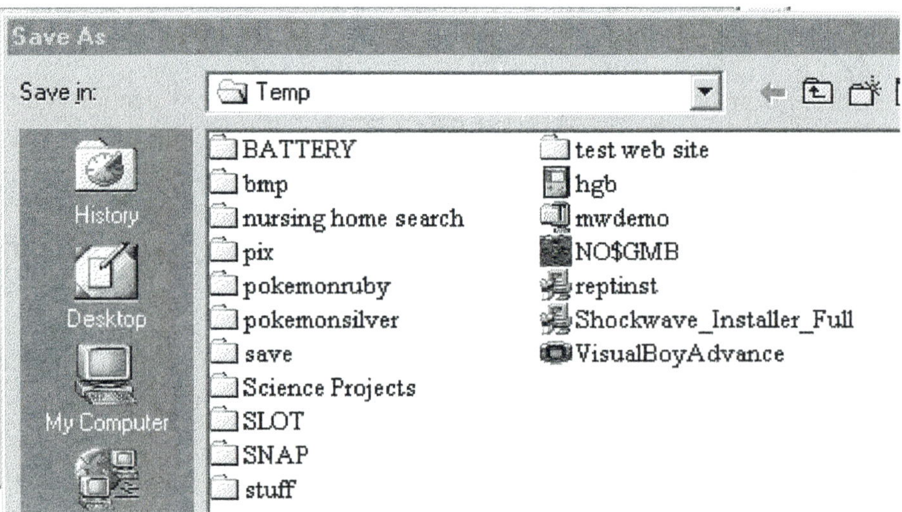

We don't want it in **Temp**, so we click on the down arrow next to the word **Temp**, and get some other alternatives. Can you find the file **C:\borland**? Choose it. Click **Save**.

Now, also download the Turbo Debugger into the **borland** folder.

Next, go to My Computer icon on the desktop and click on it, then on the **C:** folder, then on **borland**. Find the icon that looks like a box ready to open up. It says something like "freecommandlinetools." Click on it. Keep clicking to install the compiler in the **borland** folder. It will create directories for you, including one that matches the version of the compiler you have. My directory says BCC55. Yours may be a different number, like BCC62.

Now, click on the Open-Box icon for the debugger. Keep clicking **next** to install the debugger. You may need it later!

Exercises

1. Open your DOS prompt window. Change directory to the A: drive by typing **A:** at the DOS prompt. Put a floppy disk into your A: drive. See what is on it. Make a directory on it called **test**.

2. Change directory (**CD**) to your C: drive. Go to the root. If you have a directory named **C:\Temp**, open it. If you don't, make one (**MD**) and then open it ("stand in it"). Shrink the DOS window and check with Windows Explorer to see if you can see the new file. Now enlarge the DOS window.

3. Create a pathname as input for **CD** that will take you from where you are in **Temp** to the root directory. (Hint: Start with **CD ..**) Now, create another pathname as input to **CD** to go from the root directory to the **bin** directory inside your **borland** directory. Execute it. Now, type **exit** to exit the DOS prompt.

#31 Where from Here?

If you are wanting to continue now with your quest of knowledge about how computers work, here are some possibilities for you:

Buy a copy of Microsoft Visual Basic software. Learn to use it using tutorials from the Internet (I'm sorry that I can't recommend specific ones; you will have to use Google and search around.) Or, buy a book. I should warn you that this is a complex piece of software, quite different from MicroWorlds although it has some similarities.

Locate a book on C to use, on the road to Java. I looked at a number of C books for my high school class, searching for one that was readable and if possible not dull. Unfortunately, most computer books are written for adults with big vocabularies and lots of patience. Finally I found a user-friendly one that I decided would do for our high school class. It is *C for Dummies Volume I* by Dan Gookin. This book is written in an engaging style, with a lot of silliness built in. Unfortunately, it is written for adults; the jokes are occasionally mildly inappropriate (for example, one of the simple programs contains "pickup lines" for meeting a person of the opposite sex). I would not recommend this book for anyone younger than high school, and you may want to avoid it altogether. However, the alternatives are much harder to read!

If you finish your C book and want something more advanced, I would recommend a book on Java. I am recommending Java because it is becoming the "must-know" programming language for programmers these days, and is now the language for the AP computer exam. I found a Java book which is user-friendly and silly. This is *Head First Java* by Kathy Sierra and Bert Bates. It assumes some knowledge of C. This is definitely a book for high-schoolers and beyond, because of the material it covers. So any mildly inappropriate jokes could be handled by the student, I would guess. You will need your new DOS experience to install a Java compiler similar to the C compiler at that point. Run a search on Google for **java download**, and be sure your source is the program originator, Sun Microsystems.

Use the Compiler and DOS Editor

Now, if you have decided to check out *C for Dummies*, look for it used on Amazon.com. You can get it for only a few dollars. I will provide you with a little more instruction on how to use the C compiler we just installed. Unfortunately this information is not in the book!

In order to compile a program, you will need to run the C compiler from the DOS prompt. Open the DOS window and find the folder that contains the executable file, **BCC32.exe**. This path may vary depending on your download from Borland. Let's figure out what it should be.

Let's open the DOS prompt and go to the **borland** folder, and then use the **DIR** command to see what is there. We need to go into the directory called **BCC55** on my computer, possibly a higher number on yours. Once inside, do a DIR to look for the .exe file.

```
C:\borland>cd bcc55

C:\borland\BCC55>dir

 Volume in drive C has no label
 Volume Serial Number is 07D0-0A17
 Directory of C:\borland\BCC55

.                  <DIR>         01-25-04   7:16p .
..                 <DIR>         01-25-04   7:16p ..
BIN                <DIR>         01-25-04   7:16p Bin
EXAMPLES           <DIR>         01-25-04   7:16p Examples
HELP               <DIR>         01-25-04   7:16p Help
INCLUDE            <DIR>         01-25-04   7:16p Include
LIB                <DIR>         01-25-04   7:16p Lib
LICENSE  TXT           15,095    06-27-00   5:01a license.txt
README   TXT            4,510    06-27-00   5:01a readme.txt
TD32READ TXT            3,258    05-31-00   5:50a td32read.txt
TD32_L~1 TXT           15,115    05-31-00   5:50a TD32_license.txt
          4 file(s)          37,978 bytes
          7 dir(s)       7,110.34 MB free

C:\borland\BCC55>cd bin

C:\borland\BCC55\Bin>
```

Is it there? No. Let's look in the Bin folder; change directory to Bin. Run a **DIR** check again.

Yes, we see a bunch of .exe files. One is **bcc32.exe**, the compiler we will use a lot. This is our target spot! To make a pathname to this file, we have to list all the nested directories. In my case the pathname is this: **C:\Borland\BCC55\Bin.** Possibly on your computer the only difference is a higher number replacing 55. Whenever I am compiling a C program, I need to use **CD ..** to get to the root of the C drive, **C:\.** Then I need to change directory to this spot, **Bin**. I can type **CD Borland\BCC55\Bin**. So I will type this:

> **CD ..**
> **CD ..**   repeat until what I see is this: **C:\>**
> **CD Borland\BCC55\Bin**

In order to compile (process) a file, we will "stand in" Bin and type the compiler name, **bcc32**, as well as the name of the file we are wanting to compile. For instance, we could make a file called frog.c. To compile it we would type **bcc32 frog.c**. **Bcc32** is the name of the program we are running; **frog.c** is the input for the command. (*In C for Dummies*, we are choosing the option of "Borland C at the DOS prompt.")

We also need to know how to use the DOS Editor. In the book *C for Dummies*, that is how you create and change programs. Let's get used to opening it.

I will assume that you are now "standing in" the Bin directory mentioned above. Type this command: **EDIT.** The DOS Editor pops up. This is the ancestor of Notepad. It will create and edit files in the directory you are standing in (or in another one if you add a path to the name when you open and save it). It opens up with a new blank file.

Type "This is a new file." Now, we need to save it. You may be unable to use your mouse, depending on your computer. If so, use the arrow keys to move around, and press Enter to select something. Under the file menu, choose **Save**. A window pops up, including a long line of dots that you need to replace by typing a name for your file. Type **Testfile**. Press or click OK. Now you have created a file in the Bin directory. Exit the DOS Editor by selecting **File**, then **Exit**.

You'll notice that DOS menus often have a letter in each word highlighted. This shows you the keyboard shortcut for that menu item. You see the shortcut for **Exit** is **x**. So, any time you want to exit, you can press **x.** And for **Save**, press s.

Now, shrink your DOS window and use Windows Explorer to find your new file. Remember how to find Windows Explorer? Right-click on the **Start** button and choose **Explorer**. Did you find it?

Let's edit that new file. Enlarge the DOS window. Make sure you are still "standing in" Bin. Type **Edit testfile** at the prompt. The file should reappear. Now, let's try saving it in a new place. Choose **File Save As**. I will assume you have a directory called **C:\temp**. (If you don't have a **C:\temp** directory, make one by closing the DOS Editor, changing directory toward the root (**CD ..**) until you get to the root, **C:\>**. Then type **MD temp**. Now, change directories to get back to Bin.) In the series of dots for the new name, type **temp\testfile**. This puts a copy of the file in the temp directory.

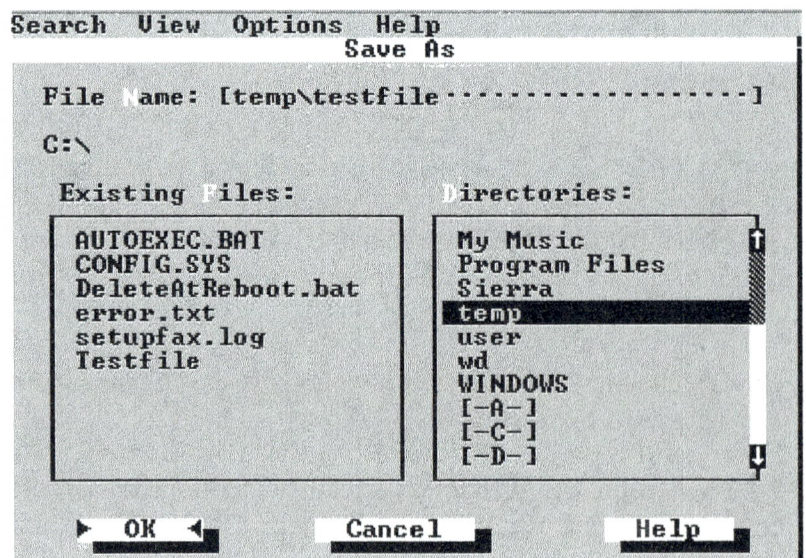

Choose OK. Exit the DOS Editor. Change directory to **temp** and see if the file is there (remember how? type **CD temp,** then **DIR**).

Exercises:

At the DOS prompt, move so you are standing in your **C:\temp** directory. Now open the DOS editor and start typing this, or some other nonsense: *The frog story continues.*

Save it with the name **frog.txt**. Now, open it again and close it again. At the DOS prompt, move to the root of the C drive, C:\. Now type **EDIT**, and open your frog file by typing its pathname from that spot: **temp\frog.txt**. Add some more to your story. Close the file.

You now have what you need to begin *C for Dummies*. If you feel uncomfortable with your level of DOS expertise, you can get a copy of *DOS for Dummies* by Dan Gookin, and work on it some more.

Appendices

Appendix I: MicroWorlds Troubleshooting and Procedure Names

Troubleshooting Guide

Make sure there are spaces between each word and between word and symbol, for example

colorunder = 15

Make sure each procedure starts with **to** and ends with **end**.

Make sure there are brackets [like these] around lists. List items are separated by spaces. For example:

setsh [horse1 horse2 horse3]

In the above example, note that the names **horse1, horse2,** and **horse3** contain no spaces.

For words used as names or nouns (not procedure names, which are actions) make sure there are double-quote marks like these **"word** , made with a single stroke of the double-quote key, or else put the words into a list with brackets. If the error message says "I don't know how to word," then you have forgotten to label **word** as a noun by using either the quote marks or the brackets. So the computer thinks it is an action word. (Or perhaps **word** is a procedure name and you have forgotten to write the procedure for **word**.)

If you can't figure out where the problem is in the program, insert some signal flags. Put lines into the code that say **show "OK** in several places. The program will print **OK** in the Command Center when it passes those spots. Then you will know where to concentrate your efforts, where it is not printing out. Remove these lines when you figure out the problem.

If your program isn't running right, it may be organized poorly. Check the logic of the sequence of things you are calling on the computer to do. If necessary, look at the answers in the answer key.

If you use a built-in procedure name by accident for one of your procedures or variable names, the program won't run right.

If you get an error message about turtles, perhaps you forgot to hatch the turtles called for.

If you use a capital O instead of a zero (0), the program won't run right.

If the error message says a procedure needs more inputs, concentrate on the line that calls that procedure and the one following, and look for the proper number of inputs and the proper number of opening and closing brackets.

If you run through this checklist and it still isn't working, try this: use **Cut** and **Paste** to move your code around on the Procedures Page. This especially works if MicroWorlds is pretending not to see one of your procedures.

Some Built-in Procedures (see Index for more):

cc clear the Command Center.

cg clears graphics.

pd puts the current turtle's pen down and requires no inputs and has no outputs.

forward or **fd** moves the current turtle in the direction its head is pointing by a number of steps. The number of steps is a required input. (**back** does the opposite).

right turns the current turtle to the right by a number of degrees. The number is a required input. (**left** does the opposite.)

wait takes one input, a number.

repeat requires two inputs: a number indicating how many repetitions, and a list of instructions to repeat. A list has brackets [ ] around it.

Presentation Mode: Go to the Gadgets menu and click on Presentation Mode. Then click the Start button. To get out of Presentation Mode, click on the black part of the screen outside of MicroWorlds.

talkto "t1 works with turtle named t1.

setc setcolor, takes a number input, sets the color the turtle is drawing.

random takes a number input, randomly produces a number less than the input.

setc random 100 will generate a random new color every time it is repeated.

fill fills the area the turtle is in with the color the turtle is set to.

seth set heading, sets the direction the turtle will move. Takes a number input. 0 is up, is to the right, -90 or 270 is to the left, 180 is down. Example: **seth 90.**

setsh, set shape, requires an input which is either a word (must be the name of a shape, such as **setsh "horse1**) or a list of words (must be a list of names of shapes). It changes the shape of the turtle. Point to a particular turtle first using **talkto.** If you give a list of shapes, the program will pick a new shape from the list every time it calls **forward** or **back.**

local reserves and names a storage place.

make puts a value in it.

show takes one input, a word or a list, and prints it on the Command Center.

: is read, "the value that is in" the storage place or variable.

ycor has as output the Ycoordinate (height on the screen) of the turtle.

xcor has as output the x coordinate (distance from the left side) of the turtle.

sety takes a number as an input and sets the Ycoordinate.

setx takes a number as input and sets the x coordinate.

launch has as an input a list of instructions [using brackets like this] to run as a separate process.

Appendix II: HTML Troubleshooting and Commands

Troubleshooting Tips:

If your HTML file doesn't display in your browser, you've forgotten one of the tags or slash marks or made some other tiny error. Enlarge Wordpad/Notepad again make the changes. Carefully go over your file, looking for pairs of tags, one to open and one to close.

The tags should be nested. That is, inside the outer pair of tags of <html> and </html> are some inner pairs, such as <body> and </body>. Between the <body> and </body> tags we might find more tag pairs, such as <p> and </p>. But we can't put a <p> tag before <body> and the corresponding </p> tag after </body>. They must be nested.

When you save your Wordpad/Notepad file, use **Save** rather than **Save As**, and type in the .html extension to the file name. You have to click on the type of file to change the way it will save, and save it as a text file. If you are using Notepad, you will probably need to type the .html file extension every time you save. If it saved as **name.html.txt**, find the file through the My Computer icon, and rename the file by right clicking on its icon. Get rid of the .txt part.

Commands

To start your page, type this:

> **<html>**
> **<head>**
> **<title> This title is the one that goes at the very top of the screen. </title>**
> **</head>**
>
> **<body>**

Change the background color. Find **<body>**. Change it to:

> **<body bgcolor="#ff0000">**

Make your headline stand out.

> **<h1> <center> This makes a centered headline in the biggest of font sizes, h1. You can also use h2 , h3, on to h6, the smallest. </h1>**

Some Paragraph Formats:

> **<p> This command gives us a new paragraph. </p>**
> **<p> <i> This gives us a new paragraph, in italic. </i> </p>**
> **<p> <b> This gives us a new paragraph, in bold type. </b> </p>**

**
 Put this in where you want to start a new line. It's called a line break.**

Don't forget these closing tags:

> **</body>**
> **</html>**

Adding Pictures

Put in picture along left side of text:

> **<p><img src="Page1.gif" ALIGN=left> Put lots of text here**
> **</p>**

Want to center the image? Don't put it in the same paragraph with the text. Make that:

> **<center> <img src="Page1.gif"></center>**
> **<p> Put text here ...</p>**

Want an image border of thickness 10 pixels? Make that:

> **<center> <img src="Page1.gif" border=10></center>**

Our image as it comes from MicroWorlds is pretty big. Want it resized? You need to specify the size in pixels. This will take some trial and error, since we don't know how big it is to begin with. The new width and height should be in the same proportion as the old, in order to keep the image looking good. Try this:

> **<img src="Page1.gif" width=300 height=200 >**

Let's align it to the right side of the page, and add some horizontal space:

> **<img src="Page1.gif" width=300 height=200 align=right hspace=20>**

This will give you an image 300 pixels wide, 200 tall, aligned to the right side of the page, and with 20 pixels of horizontal space added beside the image. (For vertical space, **vspace**.)

Links

To our own home page:

> **<a href="../index/index.html"> Go to Homepage </a>**

To an outside site:

<a href="http://www.whatevertheWebsite.com"> **Name of Web site that shows**</a>

To an email address:

<a href=mailto:name@site.com> Click here to email a question</a>

Appendix III: Bibliography

Castro, Elizabeth. *HTML for the World Wide Web, Fifth edition, With XHTML and CSS: Visual Quickstart Guide.* Berkeley, Calif.: Peachpit Press, 2003.

Corsinet: www.corsinet.com (information for animal scavenger hunt).

Gookin, Dan. *C for Dummies.* Vol. I. Foster City, Calif.: IDG Books, 1994.

Gookin, Dan. *DOS for Dummies*, 2nd ed. Foster City, Calif.: IDG Books, 1993.

Sierra, Kathy, and Bert Bates. *Head First Java.* Sebastopol, Calif.: O'Reilly & Associates, 2003.

Temple, Michael, and Hope Chafiian. "Computer Games for Kids, by Kids." *Logo Update* 7, no. 2 (Spring 1999): pages 1-5 (http://el.media.mit.edu/logo-foundation/pubs/logoupdate/v7n2/games.html)

Yoder, Sharon. *MicroWorlds 2.0: Hypermedia Project Development & Logo Scripting.* Eugene, Ore.: International Society for Technology in Education, 1997.

Appendix IV: Answers

#1 REVIEW SOLUTIONS

Make a button on Page1 using the icon that looks like a finger pushing a button. Label the button "Start." On the Procedures Page, make these procedures:

```
========
to Main
  square
end
========
to square
  pd
  repeat 4 [forward 50 right 90 wait 1]
end

to Start
  Main
end
```

VARIABLES REVIEW EXERCISES

1.
```
========
to Main
  cc
  TestVar
end
========
to Start
  Main
end

to TestVar
  local "tall
  local "short
  make "tall 60
  make "short 80
  show :tall  ; this means show the value stored in tall
  show :short
end
```

2.
```
========
to Main
  cc
  TestVar
end
========
to Start
  Main
end

to TestVar
  local "tall
  make "tall 30
  show :tall  ; this means show the value stored in tall
```

```
  make "tall 40
  show :tall
end
```

#2 MADLIBS SOLUTIONS

All the print-sentence possibilities will work. Be sure you first make a text box on Page1.

PSEUDOCODE:

```
to madlibs
;Create and name variables
;Ask the user to type in an animal name.
;Store the animal name in a variable named noun1.
;Ask the user for the name of an object.
;Store this as noun2.
;Ask the user to name something he or she likes to do.
;Store this as noun3.
;Ask the user to describe a feeling.
;Store this as adj1.
;Ask for an adverb, such as slowly, quickly, heavily, etc.
;Store this as adv1.
;Announce that here is the Madlib.
;print  "There once was a "noun1. One day the noun1 went to the
park and saw a ;noun2.  The noun1 adv1 ate the noun2 and then
went for a noun3.  After that the ;noun1 was feeling a little adj1.
Adv1 the noun1 went home and took a nap."
end
```

CODE:

```
to madlibs
  local [noun1 noun2 noun3 noun4 adj1 adv1]
   question [Please type in an animal name.]
   make "noun1 answer
   question [Please type in the name of an object.]
   make "noun2 answer
  question [Please type in the name of something you like to do.]
   make "noun3 answer
   question [Please describe a feeling.]
   make "adj1 answer
  question [Give me an adverb, such as slowly, quickly, heavily, etc.]
   make "adv1 answer
   announce [Here is your madlib.]
   print (sentence [There once was a ] :noun1 )
   print (sentence [.  One day the ] :noun1 )
   print (sentence [went to the park and saw a ] :noun2 [.])
   print (sentence [The] :noun1 [ate the ] :noun2 [and then ])
   print (sentence [went for a ] :noun3 [.])
   print (sentence [After that the ] :noun1 [was feeling a little ] :adj1
[.])
   print (sentence [Then] :adv1 [the] :noun1)
   print (sentence [went home and took a nap.])
end
```

Now, be sure you add the Main and the Start button to get a complete program:

```
to Main
  madlibs
end
```

```
to Start
  Main
end
```

#3 MADLIBS II SOLUTIONS

```
to Main
  intro
end
```

```
to intro
  question [What's your name?]; makes a dialogue box
  announce [I like your name.] ; dialogue box without space
  question [Would you like to play Madlibs? Y or N]
  if  (answer = "Y) [madlibs]
  announce "Bye!
end
```

```
to madlibs
 local [noun1 noun2 noun3 noun4 adj1 adv1]
  question [Please type in an animal name.]
  make "noun1 answer
  question [Please type in the name of an object.]
  make "noun2 answer
  question [Please type in the name of something you like to do.]
  make "noun3 answer
  question [Please describe a feeling.]
  make "adj1 answer
question [Give me an adverb, such as slowly, quickly, heavily, etc.]
  make "adv1 answer
  announce [Here is your madlib.]
  print (sentence [There once was a ] :noun1 )
  print (sentence [.  One day the ] :noun1 )
  print (sentence [went to the park and saw a ] :noun2 [.])
  print (sentence [The] :noun1 [ate the ] :noun2 [and then ])
  print (sentence [went for a ] :noun3 [.])
  print (sentence [After that the ] :noun1 [was feeling a little ] :adj1
[.])
  print (sentence [Then] :adv1 [the] :noun1)
  print (sentence  [went home and sat on the roof.])
end
```

```
to Start
  Main
end
```
FOR EXERCISE 1:

```
to intro
  question [What's your name?]; makes a dialogue box
  announce [I like your name.] ; dialogue box without space
  question [Would you like to play Madlibs? Y or N]
  ifelse  (answer = "Y) [madlibs] [announce "Bye!]
end
```

FOR EXERCISE 2, ONE QUESTION GUESSING GAME:

```
to Main
  oneq
end
```

```
to intro
  question [What's your name?]; makes a dialogue box
  announce [I like your name.] ; dialogue box without space
  question [Would you like to play One Question? Y or N]
  ifelse (answer = "y) [oneq]  [announce [Bye!]]
end
```

```
to oneq
  local "quiznumber
  make "quiznumber 4
  question [Guess a number between 0 and 10.]
  if (answer > :quiznumber) [announce  [Too big!]]
  if (answer < :quiznumber) [announce [Too small!]]
  if (answer = :quiznumber) [announce  [You got it!]]
  print (sentence [The number was] :quiznumber)
end
```

```
to Start
  Main
end
```

#4 ANIMATION USING VARIABLES SOLUTIONS

EXERCISE 2, GUESSING GAME WITH JIG ADDED:

```
to Main
  intro
end
```

```
to intro
  question [What's your name?]; makes a dialogue box
  announce [I like your name.] ; dialogue box without space
  question [Would you like to play One Question? Y or N]
  ifelse (answer = "Y) [oneq]
  [announce [Bye!]]
end
```

```
to jig
 announce [You got it!]
 talkto "t1
 pd
 repeat 30 [fd 2 wait 1 right 10 fd 4 wait 1 left 25]
end
```

```
to oneq
  local "quiznumber
  make "quiznumber 4
  question [Guess a number between 0 and 10.]
```

        if (answer > :quiznumber) [announce [Too big!]]
        if (answer < :quiznumber) [announce [Too small!]]
        if (answer = :quiznumber) [jig]
        print (sentence [The number was] :quiznumber)
end

to Start
    Main
end

#5 WANDERING TURTLE SOLUTIONS

```
to Main
   repeat 60
      [wander 5]
end
```

```
to wander :stepSize
   ; turn right by a random amount which could be negative
   right  difference random 100 50
   ; move forward by stepSize, repeat twice
   repeat 2 [forward :stepSize wait 1]
end
```

```
to Start
    Main
end
```

#5 EXERCISES

1. *Adjust the stepSize.* Change wander 5 to wander 9 or whatever.
2. *Adjust the input to make smoother lines. How do you do that?*
    Change the input to **random**. *How do you need to adjust the number
    subtracted from the random number?* Make it half the input to
    random. For example, **difference random 100 50** can become
    difference random 40 20.
3. *Put the pen down in **Main**.* Start Main with pd for pen down. See
    below.
4. *Make the turtle's shape change as it wanders around. Hint: use
    setsh in **Main**.* See below.

```
to Main
   pd
   setsh [horse1 horse2 horse3]
   repeat 60   [wander 5]
end
```

```
to Start
    Main
end
```

```
to wander :stepSize
   ; turn right by a random amount which could be negative
   right difference random 100 50
   ; move forward by stepSize, repeat twice
   repeat 2 [forward :stepSize wait 1]
end
```

#6 ENHANCED WANDERING TURTLE SOLUTIONS

EXERCISE 5

```
to wander :stepSize :dizziness
   ; turn right by a random amount which could be negative
   ; turn right by a random amount up to dizziness
   right difference random :dizziness  quotient :dizziness 2
   ; move forward by stepSize, repeat twice
   repeat 2 [forward :stepSize wait 1]
end
```

#8 MAZE II: WIN OR LOSE?

A basic maze:

**Create a button labeled "go." Draw a maze using thick red lines from
the drawing center (under the paintbrush icon).**

```
to Main
   talkto "t1
   launch [repeat 2000 [forward 3 direct readchar ] ]
   waituntil [colorunder = 15]
   announce [You lose!]
   reset
end
```

```
to direct :key
   if (ascii :key) = 28 [seth 270 fd 1]
   if (ascii :key) = 29 [seth 90 fd 1]
   if (ascii :key) = 30 [seth 0 fd 1]
   if (ascii :key) = 31 [seth 180 fd 1]
   if (ascii :key) = 37 [seth 270 fd 1]
   if (ascii :key) = 39 [seth 90 fd 1]
   if (ascii :key) = 38 [seth 0 fd 1]
   if (ascii :key) = 40 [seth 180 fd 1]
   if (:key = "s) [stopall]
end
```

```
to go
   Main
end
```

```
to reset
   talkto "t1
   setpos [-319 -164]
   seth 0
end
```

EXERCISES:

1. Use the turtle-hatching button to place a new turtle at the destination
    point in the maze. This is t2.

2. Add underlined lines:

```
to Main
  talkto "t1
  setsh 0
  launch [repeat 2000 [forward 3 direct readchar ] ]
  when [touching? "t1 "t2] [setsh "dog1 ]
  waituntil [colorunder = 15]
  announce [You lose!]
  reset
end
```

Flow chart addition:

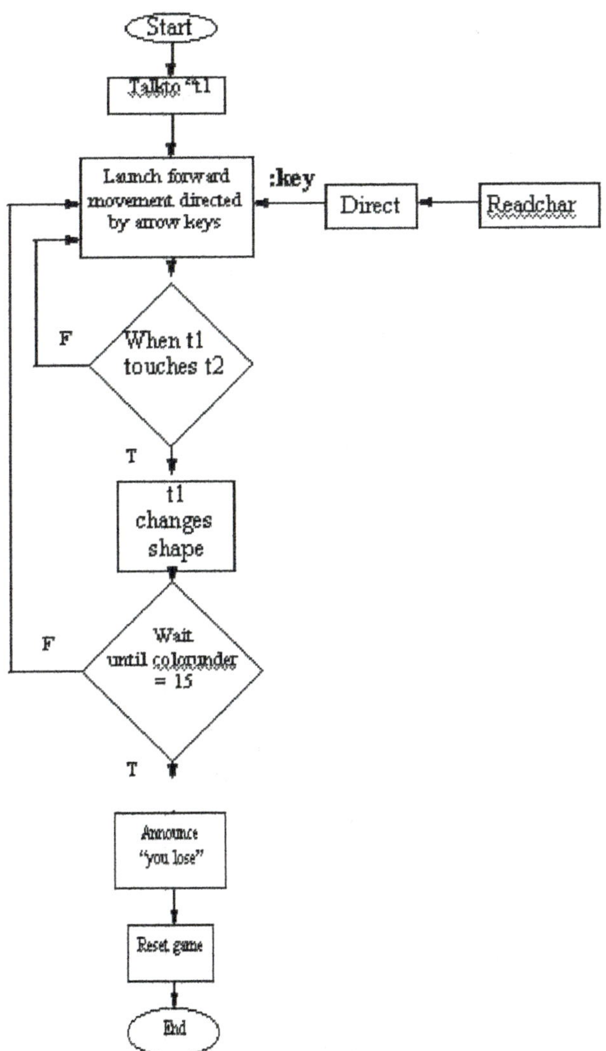

3. Turtle 1 changes to random shapes when it hits the castle:

```
to Main
  talkto "t1
  launch [repeat 2000 [forward 3 direct readchar ] ]
  when [touching? "t1 "t2] [win]
  waituntil [colorunder = 15]
  announce [You lose!]
  reset
end
```

```
to direct :key
  if (ascii :key) = 28 [seth 270 fd 1]
  if (ascii :key) = 29 [seth 90 fd 1]
  if (ascii :key) = 30 [seth 0 fd 1]
  if (ascii :key) = 31 [seth 180 fd 1]
  if (ascii :key) = 37 [seth 270 fd 1]
  if (ascii :key) = 39 [seth 90 fd 1]
  if (ascii :key) = 38 [seth 0 fd 1]
  if (ascii :key) = 40 [seth 180 fd 1]
  if (:key = "s) [stopall]
end
to go
  Main
end

to win
  announce [You win!]
  talkto "t1
  setsh "cloud wait 2
  setsh random 60 wait 10
end

to reset
  talkto "t1
  setpos [-319 -164]
end
```

4. Change **win** to this, adding underlined line:

```
to win
  announce [You win!]
  talkto "t1
  setsh "cloud wait 2
  setsh random 60 wait 10
  reset
end
```

Change reset to this, adding underlined line:

```
to reset
  talkto "t1
  setpos [-319 -164]
  seth 0
  setsh "turtle
end
```

5. Add flow chart to describe what we have so far:

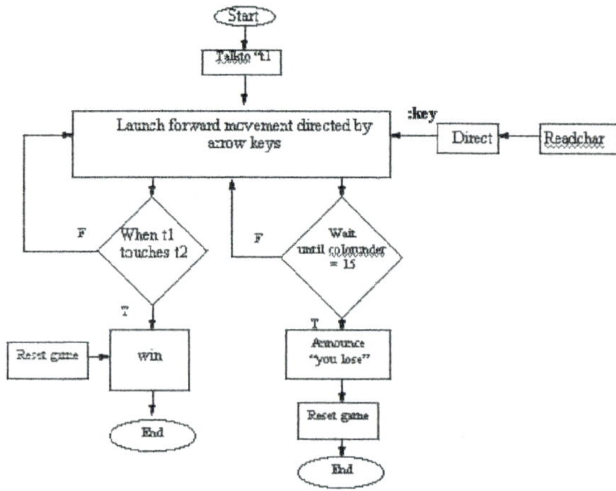

PRINCE/PRINCESS PROJECT: Game asks the user whether the user would rather be a prince or a princess, and the turtle turns into a boy or girl when it gets to the castle:

```
to Main
  local "preference
  announce [Hi!   If you get to the castle, you will be changed back into a human.]
  question [Would you like to be a prince or a princess? B for boy or G for girl]
  ifelse (answer = "B) [make "preference 41] [make "preference 40]
  talkto "t1
  launch [repeat 2000 [forward 3 direct readchar ] ]
  when [touching? "t1 "t2] [win :preference]
  waituntil [colorunder = 15]
  announce [You lose!]
  reset
end
```

```
to direct :key
  if (ascii :key) = 28 [seth 270 fd 1]
  if (ascii :key) = 29 [seth 90 fd 1]
  if (ascii :key) = 30 [seth 0 fd 1]
  if (ascii :key) = 31 [seth 180 fd 1]
  if (ascii :key) = 37 [seth 270 fd 1]
  if (ascii :key) = 39 [seth 90 fd 1]
  if (ascii :key) = 38 [seth 0 fd 1]
  if (ascii :key) = 40 [seth 180 fd 1]
  if (:key = "s) [stopall]
end
```

```
to win :gender
  announce [You win!]
  talkto "t1
  setsh "cloud wait 2
  setsh :gender wait 10
  reset
end
```

```
to go
  Main
end
```

```
to reset
  talkto "t1
  setpos [-319 -164]
  seth 0
  setsh "turtle
end
```

#9 MAZE III

```
to Main
  talkto "t1
  launch [repeat 2000 [forward 3 direct readchar ] ]
  talkto "t3
  launch [repeat 2000 [forward 3 wait 1]]
  when [colorunder = 15] [right 190]
  talkto "t4
  launch [repeat 2000 [forward 3 wait 1]]
  when [colorunder = 15] [right 190]

  talkto "t1
  when [colorunder = 15] [lose]
  when [touching? "t1 "t2] [win]
  when [touching? "t1 "t3] [lose]
  when [touching? "t1 "t4] [lose]
end
```

```
to direct :key
  if (ascii :key) = 28 [seth 270 fd 1]
  if (ascii :key) = 29 [seth 90 fd 1]
  if (ascii :key) = 30 [seth 0 fd 1]
  if (ascii :key) = 31 [seth 180 fd 1]
  if (ascii :key) = 37 [seth 270 fd 1]
  if (ascii :key) = 39 [seth 90 fd 1]
  if (ascii :key) = 38 [seth 0 fd 1]
  if (ascii :key) = 40 [seth 180 fd 1]
  if (:key = "s) [stopall]
end
```

```
to go
  Main
end
```

```
to lose
  announce [You lose!]
  wait 5
  reset
end
```

```
to reset
  talkto "t1
  setpos [-319 -164]
  seth 0
  setsh "turtle
end
```

```
to win
  announce [You win!]
  talkto "t1
  setsh "cloud wait 2
  setsh random 60 wait 10
  reset
end
```

#10 MAZE IV

```
to Maineasy
  talkto "t1
  launch [repeat 2000 [forward 3 direct readchar ] ]
  talkto "t3
  launch [repeat 2000 [forward 3 wait 3]]
  when [colorunder = 15] [right 190]
  talkto "t4
  launch [repeat 2000 [forward 3 wait 3]]
  when [colorunder = 15] [right 190]
  talkto "t1
  when [colorunder = 15] [lose]
  when [touching? "t1 "t2] [win]
  when [touching? "t1 "t3] [lose]
  when [touching? "t1 "t4] [lose]
end

to Mainmedium
  talkto "t1
  launch [repeat 2000 [forward 3 direct readchar ] ]
  talkto "t3
  launch [repeat 2000 [forward 3 wait 2]]
  when [colorunder = 15] [right 190]
  talkto "t4
  launch [repeat 2000 [forward 3 wait 2]]
  when [colorunder = 15] [right 190]
  talkto "t1
  when [colorunder = 15] [lose]
  when [touching? "t1 "t2] [win]
  when [touching? "t1 "t3] [lose]
  when [touching? "t1 "t4] [lose]
end

to Mainhard
  talkto "t1
  launch [repeat 2000 [forward 3 direct readchar ] ]
  talkto "t3
  launch [repeat 2000 [forward 4 wait 2]]
  when [colorunder = 15] [right 190]
  talkto "t4
  launch [repeat 2000 [forward 4 wait 2]]
  when [colorunder = 15] [right 190]
  talkto "t1
  when [colorunder = 15] [lose]
  when [touching? "t1 "t2] [win]
  when [touching? "t1 "t3] [lose]
  when [touching? "t1 "t4] [lose]
end
```

```
to direct :key
  if (ascii :key) = 28 [seth 270 fd 1]
  if (ascii :key) = 29 [seth 90 fd 1]
  if (ascii :key) = 30 [seth 0 fd 1]
  if (ascii :key) = 31 [seth 180 fd 1]
  if (ascii :key) = 37 [seth 270 fd 1]
  if (ascii :key) = 39 [seth 90 fd 1]
  if (ascii :key) = 38 [seth 0 fd 1]
  if (ascii :key) = 40 [seth 180 fd 1]
  if (:key = "s) [stopall]
end

to easy
  easypage
  Maineasy
end

to hard
  hardpage
  Mainhard
end

to index
  Page1
end

to lose
  announce [You lose!]
  wait 5
  reset
end

to medium
  mediumpage
  Mainmedium
end

to reset
  talkto "t1
  setpos [-319 -164]
  seth 0
  setsh "turtle
end

to win
  announce [You win!]
  talkto "t1
  setsh "cloud wait 2
  setsh random 60 wait 10
  reset
end
```

#10 MAZE IV

EXERCISES

1. *Add teleporter booths. Here's how: put a box of another color into
   the maze. When the t1 turtle hits the color, it jumps to a different spot
   in the maze. To find the coordinates of the spot you want to teleport
   to, move the turtle there using the mouse, and then type* **show pos** *in
   the Command Center.*

Make a sky blue box (color is 95) somewhere in your medium maze.
Mainmedium will contain this section, with new line underlined:

```
talkto "t1
   when [colorunder = 15] [lose]
   when [colorunder =  95] [setpos 18 –146]
   when [touching? "t1 "t2] [win]
```

*2. Create animations using a list of shapes with **setsh** and repeated calls to forward.*

Have the t1 turtle animate when it reaches the goal. Add underlined lines:

```
to win
   announce [You win!]
   talkto "t1
   setsh "cloud wait 2
   setsh random 60 wait 10
   setsh [horse1 horse2 horse3]
   seth 90
   repeat 10 [forward 1 wait 1]
   reset
end
```

*Make an animation for the spiders (**t3** and **t4**) as they move, giving realistic motion.* Add underlined lines:

```
to Maineasy
   talkto "t1
   launch [repeat 2000 [forward 3 direct readchar] ]
   talkto "t3
   setsh [bee1 bee2]
   launch [repeat 2000 [forward 3 wait 3]]
   when [colorunder = 15] [right 190]
   talkto "t4
   setsh [bee1 bee2]
   launch [repeat 2000 [forward 3 wait 3]]
   when [colorunder = 15] [right 190]
   ...
```

Animate the t1 turtle as it goes through the maze. One possibility: make it look like Pac-Man. an ancient videogame hero who looks like a yellow cookie. You can make new shapes by double-clicking on the blank shapes in the shape center. and using drawing tools to construct them. Construct shapes and call them pac1. pac2. and pac3, for example. Then add underlined line:

```
to Maineasy
   talkto "t1
   setsh [pac1 pac2 pac3 pac2]
   launch [repeat 2000 [forward 3 direct readchar] ]
   ...
```

#11 RACE I

Save your sketch to compare to the flow chart in the next lesson.

#12 RACE II

Note,: You may need to thicken your finish line.
=================

```
to Main
 setup
 question [Player 1, What is the height of Mount Everest in miles?]
 ifelse (answer = "6)
       [talkto "t1 fd 170][announce [Wrong answer!  It was 6.]]
 wait 5
 question [Player 2, What is the depth of the Marianas Trench in miles?]
 ifelse (answer = "6)
       [talkto "t2 fd 170] [announce [Wrong answer!  It was 6.]]
 wait 5
question [Player 1, What is the mountain range of Mt. Everest?]
 ifelse (answer = "Himalayas )
       [talkto "t1 fd 170] [announce [Wrong answer!  It was Himalayas.]]
 wait 5
 question [Player 2, What is the word for a monk in Tibet?]
 ifelse (answer = "Lama)
        [talkto "t2 fd 170] [announce [Wrong answer!  It was Lama.]]
 wait 5
 question [Player 1,What man from India inspired Martin Luther King Jr.?]
 ifelse (answer = "Gandhi)
       [talkto "t1 fd 170] [announce [Wrong answer!  It was Gandhi.]]
 wait 5
 question [Player 2, What is the main religion in India?]
 ifelse (answer = "Hinduism)
       [talkto "t2 fd 170] [announce [Wrong answer!  It was Hinduism.]]
 wait 5
question [Player 1, What is the main religion in Pakistan and Bangladesh?]
  ifelse (answer = "Islam)
        [talkto "t1 fd 170][announce [Wrong answer!  It was Islam.]]
 wait 5
 question [Player 2, in what country is Mount Everest?]
 ifelse (answer = "Nepal)
       [talkto "t2 fd 170][announce [Wrong answer! It was Nepal.]]
 wait 5
 talkto [t1 t2]
 if (colorunder = 15)[ win]
end
```
===============

```
   to win
      talkto "t3
      st; shows turtle
      setsh [bee1 bee2]
      repeat 30 [forward .01 wait 2]
   end

   to setup
      talkto "t1
      setpos [-346 -73]
      seth 90
      talkto "t2
      setpos [-346 -151]
      seth 90
      talkto "t3
      ht ;hides turtle
      setpos [340 -117]
      seth 90
   end
```

to Start
    Main
    end

EXERCISE:
Change this line at the end of **Main**:
    ifelse (colorunder = 15)[win] [announce [No winners!]]
    end

#13 RACE III

Change this procedure:
    to win
    Page2
    announce[You win!!!!!]
    talkto [t1 t2 t3 t4 t5 t6 t7 t8 t9]
    setsh [ball1 fire1 fire2 fire3]
    repeat 30 [forward .01 wait 2]
    end
Change this procedure:
    to setup
    Page1
    talkto "t1
    setpos [-346 -73]
    seth 90
    talkto "t2
    setpos [-346 -151]
    seth 90
    talkto "t3
    ht ;hides turtle
    setpos [340 -117]
    seth 90
    end

#14 HANGMAN I: GOING LOOPY

EXERCISE 1: Be sure you have a stopall button and a Start button.
    ================
    to Main
      pd
      forever
      [
        talkto "t1
        seth 0 forward 40 wait 1
        right 170 forward 40 wait 1
      ]
    end
    ================
    to Start
      Main
    end

EXERCISE 2
    to Main
      local "counter
      make "counter 0

    pd
    forever
    [
      talkto "t1
      seth 0 forward 40 wait 1
      right 170 forward 40 wait 1
      show :counter
      make "counter sum :counter 1
    ]
    end

EXERCISE 3 Hatch two more turtles.
    ================
    to Main
      local "counter
      make "counter 0
      pd
      forever
      [
        talkto "t1
        seth 0 forward 40 wait 1
        right 170 forward 40 wait 1
        show :counter
        make "counter sum :counter 1
        if (:counter = 10) [talkto "t2 seth -90 setsh [bird1 bird2] repeat
3 [forward 3 wait 1]]
        if (:counter = 20) [talkto "t3 seth 90 setsh [bee1 bee2] repeat 3
[forward 3 wait 1]]
        if (:counter = 30) [stopall]
      ]
    end
    ================
    to Start
      Main
    end

EXERCISE 4
Replace the three if statements with these:

    when [:counter = 10] [talkto "t2 seth -90 setsh [bird1 bird2]
            repeat 3 [forward 3 wait 1]]
    when [:counter = 20] [talkto "t3 seth 90 setsh [bee1 bee2]
            repeat 3 [forward 3 wait 1]]
    when [:counter = 30] [stopall]

This doesn't work because we can't have lots of processes running at the
same time working on the same set of numbers (the counters).

#15 HANGMAN II

    ================
    to Main
      local "counter
      make "counter 0

      forever
      [
      question [Please give me a letter]

    if (answer = "d) [talkto "text1 print answer]
    if (answer = "o) [talkto "text2 print answer]
    if (answer = "g) [talkto "text3 print answer]
    show :counter
    if not (or answer = "d answer = "o answer = "g)
      [make "counter sum :counter 1]
    if (:counter = 6)[stopall]

    ]
end
===========

to Start
  Main
end

Exercises
1: F
2: T
3: T
4: F

#16 HANGMAN III

EXERCISE 1
=========

```
to Main
  local [counter letter1 letter2 letter3]
  reset
  make "counter 0
  forever
  [
   question [Please give me a letter]
   if (answer = "d) [talkto "text1 print answer make "letter1
answer]
   if (answer = "o) [talkto "text2 print answer make "letter2
answer]
   if (answer = "g) [talkto "text3 print answer make "letter3
answer]
   show :counter
if  not ( or answer = "d answer = "o answer = "g) [make "counter
sum :counter 1]
   if (:counter = 6)[announce [You lose!] stopall]
   if (and :letter1 = "d :letter2 = "o :letter3 = "g)[announce [You
win!] stopall]

   ]
end
```
===========

```
to reset
  talkto "text1
  cleartext
  talkto "text2
  cleartext
  talkto "text3
  cleartext
end

to Start
  Main
end
```

#17 HANGMAN IV
=========

```
to Main
  local [counter letter1 letter2 letter3]
  talkto [t1 t2 t3 t4 t5 t6]
  ht
  reset
  make "counter 0
  forever
  [
   question [Please give me a letter]
if (answer = "d) [talkto "text1 print answer make "letter1 answer]
if (answer = "o) [talkto "text2 print answer make "letter2 answer]
if (answer = "g) [talkto "text3 print answer make "letter3 answer]
show :counter
if  not ( or answer = "d answer = "o answer = "g)
        [make "counter sum :counter 1]
   if (:counter = 1) [talkto "t2 st setsh "noose]
   if (:counter = 2) [talkto "t1 st setsh "head]
   if (:counter = 3) [talkto "t3 st setsh "body]
   if (:counter = 4) [talkto "t5 st setsh "arm2]
   if (:counter = 5) [talkto "t4 st setsh "arm1]
   if (:counter = 6) [talkto "t6 st setsh "legs]
   if (:counter = 6)[announce [You lose!] stopall]
   if (and :letter1 = "d :letter2 = "o :letter3 = "g)
          [announce [You win!] stopall]

   ]
end
```
===========

```
to Start
  Main
end

to reset
  talkto "text1
  cleartext
  talkto "text2
  cleartext
  talkto "text3
  cleartext
end
```

EXERCISE 1: Change underlined lines.

```
to Main
  local [counter letter1 letter2 letter3]
  talkto [t1 t2 t3 t4 t5 t6]
  ht
  reset
  make "counter 0
  forever
  [
   question [Please give me a letter]
   if (answer = "d)
          [talkto "text1 print answer make "letter1 answer]
```

```
    if (answer = "o)
        [talkto "text2 print answer make "letter2 answer]
    if (answer = "g)
        [talkto "text3 print answer make "letter3 answer]
    show :counter
    if  not ( or answer = "d answer = "o answer = "g)
        [make "counter sum :counter 1]
    if (:counter = 1) [talkto "t2 st setsh "noose]
    if (:counter = 2) [talkto "t1 st setsh "head]
    if (:counter = 3) [talkto "t3 st setsh "body]
    if (:counter = 4) [talkto "t5 st setsh "arm2]
    if (:counter = 5) [talkto "t4 st setsh "arm1]
    if (:counter = 6) [talkto "t6 st setsh "legs]
    if (:counter = 6)
        [announce [You lose!] talkto "t1 st setsh "deadguy
        stopall]
    if (and :letter1 = "d :letter2 = "o :letter3 = "g)
        [announce [You win!] stopall]

    ]
end
```

EXERCISE 2: Change this line near the end of Main, adding "win":

```
    if (and :letter1 = "d :letter2 = "o :letter3 = "g)
            [announce [You win!] win stopall]
```

Add this procedure:

```
to win
  talkto [t2 t3 t4 t5 t6]
  ht
  talkto "t1
  setsh [fire1 fire2]
  repeat 30 [forward 0.01 wait 1]
end
```

#18 CITY I

```
========
to Main
  talkto "t1
  st
  question [I will build you a house.  Do you want big or small?]
  ifelse (answer = "big) [house 1][house 0.5]
  wait 5
  question [Do  you want 1 or 2 windows?]
  ifelse (answer = 1) [1window][2window]
  wait 5
  question [Do you want red or blue?]
  ifelse (answer = "red)[fillred][fillblue]
  pu sety -125 seth 90 forward 125 ;move down the street a ways
  question [Do you want to draw another house? Y or N]
  ifelse (answer = "Y)[Main][animate]
end
========

to start
 cg
 setup
 Main
end
```

```
to house :size  ;this procedure doesn't actually use the variable yet
  seth 0
  pd repeat 4[forward 50 right 90] ;a square
  pu seth 0 forward 50 right 30 pd ;move to roof
  repeat 3[forward 50 right 120 wait 1] ;triangle
  pu seth 180 forward 50 left 90 forward 20 seth 0 ;move to door
 pd repeat 2 [forward 20 right 90 forward 10 right 90 wait 1] ;door
  pu seth 90 forward 13 left 90 forward 30  ;move to window
end

to 1window
  pd repeat 4[forward 15 right 90]
end

to 2window
  pd repeat 4[forward 15 right 90]
  pu seth -90 forward 25 seth 0
  pd repeat 4[forward 15 right 90]
end

to fillred
  setc 15
  pu seth -100 forward 3 pd
  fill
end

to fillblue
  setc 105
  pu seth -100 forward 3 pd
  fill
end

to setup
  talkto "t1
  pu  ;pen up
  setpos [-359 -125]
 end

to animate
end
```

EXERCISE: Here is a preliminary version that uses **forever** to make the loop. It also doesn't animate or re-size the house yet:

```
========
to Main
  forever
  [
  talkto "t1
  st
  question [I will build you a house.  Do you want big or small?]
  ifelse (answer = "big) [house 1][house 0.5]
  wait 5
  question [Do  you want 1 or 2 windows?]
  ifelse (answer = 1) [1window][2window]
  wait 5
  question [Do you want red or blue?]
```

```
ifelse (answer = "red)[fillred][fillblue]
pu sety -125 seth 90 forward 125 ;move down the street a ways
question [Do you want to draw another house? Y or N]
if (answer = "N)[animate]
]
end
```

========

All other procedures are the same except for this one:

```
to animate
  stopall
end
```

#19 CITY II

========

```
to Main
  local "hsize
  talkto "t1
  st
  question [I will build you a house.  Do you want big or small?]
  ifelse (answer = "big) [house 1 make "hsize 1]
    [house 0.5 make "hsize 0.5]
  wait 5
  question [Do  you want 1 or 2 windows?]
  ifelse (answer = 1) [1window :hsize][2window :hsize]
  wait 5
  question [Do you want red or blue?]
  ifelse (answer = "red)[fillred][fillblue]
  pu sety -125 seth 90 forward 125 * :hsize ;move down the street
  question [Do you want to draw another house? Y or N]
  ifelse (answer = "Y)[Main][animate]
end
```

========

```
to start
  cg
  setup
  Main
end
```

```
to house :size
  seth 0
  pd repeat 4[forward 50 * :size right 90] ;a square
  pu seth 0 forward 50 * :size right 30 pd ;move to roof
  repeat 3[forward 50 * :size right 120 wait 1] ;triangle
  pu seth 180 forward 50 * :size left 90 forward 20 * :size seth 0
;move to door
  pd repeat 2 [forward 20 * :size right 90 forward 10 * :size right 90
wait 1]  ;door
  pu seth 90 forward 13 * :size left 90 forward 30 * :size
;move to window
  end
```

```
to 1window :w1size
  pd repeat 4[forward 15 * :w1size right 90]
end
```

```
to 2window :w2size
```

```
  pd repeat 4[forward 15 * :w2size right 90]
  pu seth -90 forward 25 * :w2size seth 0
  pd repeat 4[forward 15 * :w2size right 90]
end
```

```
to fillred
  setc 15
  pu seth -100 forward 3 pd
  fill
end
```

```
to fillblue
  setc 105
  pu seth -100 forward 3 pd
  fill
end
```

```
to setup
  talkto "t1
  pu ;pen up
  setpos [-359 -125]
end
```

```
to animate
end
```

#20 CITY III

Make these changes to setup and animate:

```
to setup
  talkto "t1
  pu ;pen up
  setpos [-359 -125]
  talkto [t2 t3 t4 t5]
  pu ht ;pen up, hide turtle
  setpos [-359 -130]
end
```

```
to animate
  talkto "t2
  st seth 90 ;show turtle, set heading to face right
  setsh [walker1 walker2 walker3]
  launch [repeat 5000 [forward 2 wait 1]]
  talkto "t3
  st seth 90
  setsh [jeep1 jeep2]
  launch [repeat 5000 [forward 3 wait 1]]
  talkto "t4
  st seth 90
  setsh [horse1 horse2 horse3]
  launch [repeat 5000 [forward 5 wait 1]]
  talkto "t5
  st seth 90
  setsh [skater1 skater2 skater3]
  launch [repeat 5000 [forward 3 wait 2]]
end
```

21 INTERNET SCAVENGER HUNT: ODD FACTS ON ANIMALS

Students must also provide a unique URL for each answer. URLs will vary.

1. Up to a week.
2. A young chicken 5 to 6 weeks of age
3. About 500,000 eggs
4. About 1 inch
5. A nocturnal European weasel.
6. Over 6 billion dust mites
7. Twenty times a second
8. All clams start out as males
9. Syria, 1930
10. Amazon ants (red ants found in the western U.S.)
11. Up to five miles away
12. The shortest is the American opossum, 12 to 13 days; the longest is the Asiatic elephant, taking 608 days, or just over 20 months, nearly two years.
13. The blue whale.
14. Beaver teeth
15. Camels have three eyelids.
16. Chameleons
17. The greyhound breed
18. 50 to 60 mph
19. Hens' bodies need about 24 to 26 hours to produce one egg. After thirty minutes of rest, they start making an egg again.
20. 1/12th teaspoon
21. Kittens
22. Seven years
23. Penguins
24. 300 feet of earth
25. About 15 years.
26. Tubular.
27. Sharks. They are apparently immune even to cancer.

22 INTERNET SCAVENGER HUNT: GEOGRAPHY

Students should also include a unique URL for each answer. URLs will vary.

1. Danish & Faroese
2. Ch'in
3. Dalai Lama
4. Kaje /buwa
5. Roman
6. Portugal
7. Almaty
8. Karakum, Kyzylkum
9. Iran
10. Iraq
11. Georgia, Armenia, and Azerbaijan
12. The Soviet Union
13. Indus River Valley
14. Phoenicians
15. Tunisia
16. Dido
17. Hokkaido, Honshu, Shikoku, and Kyushu
18. Myanmar
19. Land of the Free
20. Borneo
21. Indonesia
22. Luzon and Mindanao
23. Magellan

#30 THE NEXT STEP: DOS

EXERCISE 1:

A:
MD test
EXERCISE 2:

C:
Repeat" **CD ..** " until you are at C:\

CD temp
If you get an error message, do this:
MD temp
CD temp
Now you are standing in the temp directory. To see it in Windows, right-click on the Start button and select Explore. Now find the folder Temp in the C: folder. Do you see it? Now enlarge the DOS window.

EXERCISE 3:

CD ..
CD borland\BCC55\bin
(the 55 may be a different number for you)

exit

Index

and, 84, 91
animation, 56, 103
animations, 65
announce, 18
answer, 14
ascii, 43
Average, 136
background, 121, 159
background picture, 66
bandwidth, 126
batch file, 152
Boolean, 21, 84
browser, 118
C programming language, 149
cc, 10, 158
CD, 146
cell, 131
cg, 158
Children, vi
Children, Internet safety, vi
clear contents, 134
clear the Command Center, 11
code, 19
colorunder, 51, 157
Command Center, 3, 17
compiler, 149
Composer, 118
Composer, Mozilla, 125
coordinates, 55, 65, 70, 98
copy, 121
copyright, 121
counter, 73
cut and **paste**, 157
default Web page, 127
difference, 30
DIR, 146
directions, 72
divide, 38
Domain hosting, 126
domain name, 126
domain registrations, 126
DOS, 143
drawing center, 42, 49
duplicate page, 63, 72
edit-paste, 121
email accounts, 126
equals sign, 91
error codes, spread sheet, 134
exe, 6
file transfer protocol, or FTP, 127

fill, 158
fill down, 133
flow chart, 42
forever, 75
Format spread sheets, 141
formula pane, 132, 139
forward, 3, 158
free image, 122
FTP, 127
FTP, drag and drop, 127
functions, spread sheet, 136
goals, 4
google, 122
Google, 108
GUI, 143
headline, 159
headline, HTML, 113
hide turtle, 92
house, 98
HTML, 111
HTML commands, 159
HTML Troubleshooting & Commands, **159**
HTML troubleshooting tips, **159**
if, 77
IF, spreadsheet, 138
ifelse, 23
if-then statement, 21
image for Web page, 114
image from the Internet, 66
image, Web page, 160
images vanishing, 122
independent process, 103
index page, 63
infinite loop, 99
input, 4, 26
insert column, 138
insert row, 138
instruction, 4
instructions, 3
Internet, 107
Internet Safety for Children, vi
Internet, put MicroWorlds work on, 65
launch, 47, 75, 158
Launch, 103
link, Web page, 116
links, 119, 121
Links, 160
local, 17, 158
Local, 7
loop, 95

loops, 73
Mailbox, 7
make, 7, 14, 158
MD, 147
MicroWorlds 2.0, vii
MicroWorlds Built-in Procedures, **158**
MicroWorlds EX, vii
MicroWorlds Help, **157**
MicroWorlds troubleshooting, 157
Minimum Computer Requirements, vi
Mozilla Composer, 118
MS-DOS, 143
multiple pages, 63
name page, 63
not, 84
Notepad, 111
or, 84, 85
Page1, **vii**, 5
Page2, 72
Pages menu, 63
parameter, 37
parental controls, vi
pathname, 149
pd, 3, 158
POP3, 126
presentation mode, 22
Presentation Mode, 72, 158
print, 15
procedures, 4
Procedures Page, **vii**, 5
program, 3
pseudocode, 13, 33
Pseudocode, 19
question, 14, 69, 70
quotient, 38
random, 158
Random, 29
RD, 148
readchar, 43
repeat, 6, 73, 158
right, 3, 32, 158
Safety, vi
Sandbox, 13
Save image from Internet, 122
search application, 143
search engine, 107
search your PC, 114

sentence, 16
setc setcolor, 158
seth, 158
Setpos, 55
setsh, 56, 157, 158
setx, 158
sety, 98, 158
shape creation, 57
shape name, 56
shapes, viii
show, 9, 76, 157, 158
show pos, 55, 70, 98
show turtle, 92
slider, 62
spread sheet, 131
spread sheet formulas (equations), 131
spyware, 107
square, 5
stopall, 77
sum, 134
table, HTML, 119
tags, 111
talkto, 71, 158
template, 119
template, Web site, 127
text box, 15, 62, 79
title, 159
title, Web page, 125
touching?, 55
troubleshooting, 76
Troubleshooting HTML, 159
Troubleshooting MicroWorlds, **157**
turtle, 57
URL, 108
variable, 100
variables, 6, 89, 95, 97
viruses, 107
wait, 6, 158
waituntil, 52
Web site templates, 126
webplayer plug-in, 65
What You See Is What You Get, 118
when, 55, 57, 77
Windows Explorer, 148
Wordpad, 111
xcor, 158
ycor, 158

ORDER PAGE

Available from Motherboard Books:

Computer Science Pure and Simple Book 1

Computer Science Pure and Simple Book 2

MicroWorlds 2.0 disk from LCSI

To order from Motherboard Books,
go to www.motherboardbooks.com
or mail to

Motherboard Books
PO Box 430041
St. Louis, MO 63143